SKINHEAD STREET GANGS

Special thanks for the help and advice to Oregon State Trooper Griff Holland—cop, partner, skinhead gang expert, and friend.

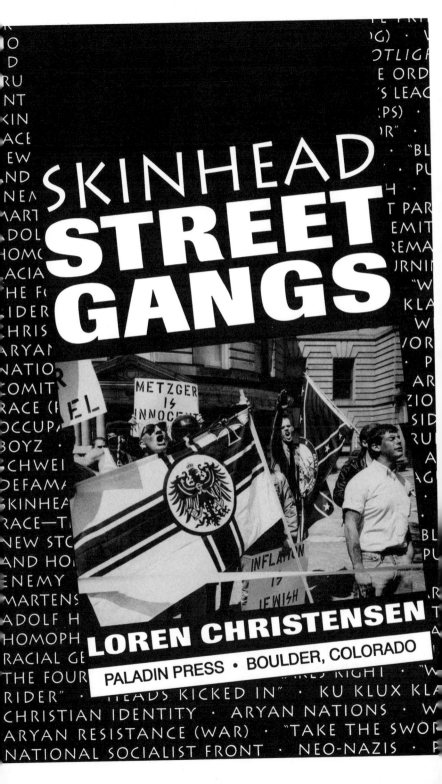

Also by Loren Christensen:

Anything Goes: Practical Karate for the Streets

The Way Alone: Your Path to Excellence in the Martial Arts

The Way of the Warrior: The Violent Side

Winning with American Kata: The New Breed of Competitors

Skinhead Street Gangs
by Loren Christensen

Copyright © 1994 by Loren Christensen

ISBN 0-87364-756-4
Printed in the United States of America

Published by Paladin Press, a division of
Paladin Enterprises, Inc., P.O. Box 1307,
Boulder, Colorado 80306, USA.
(303) 443-7250

Direct inquiries and/or orders to the above address.

CONTENTS

had just gotten transferred off the street to be a crime analyst specialist at Central, the downtown police precinct in Portland, Oregon. It was late 1987, and I was well into my fifteenth year with the Portland Police Bureau. Black, Asian, white, and Hispanic gangs were just beginning to rear their ugly heads in Portland, but as with many cities, the political powers-that-be were actively denying that it was happening in the town known affectionately as "The City of Roses." This denial continued for months, despite the fact that street officers were dealing with gangs on a daily basis.

In order to take a proactive stance, one lieutenant took it upon himself to direct the crime analyst people at each precinct to be responsible for monitoring the activity of specific gangs. The analyst at North Precinct was told to monitor the Bloods, Crips, and Hispanics; the East Precinct analyst was to monitor the Southeast Asian gangs; and I was assigned skinheads at Central Precinct. The arrangement was fine with me because skinhead activity at that time was low compared to the other gangs, and I already had enough to do without the extra work.

But in early 1988, after an Asian man was beaten by skinheads in front of his family on a downtown street corner, the press immediately wanted to know who these bald thugs were and what they were all about. Since the officers working in the intelligence division didn't want their names and pictures in the media, I was directed to answer all requests for information.

The media like to be able to say that their information source is an expert. The problem was, I didn't know anything about white supremacy or neo-Nazi skinheads. Up to that point I had just been reading street officers' reports and dropping them into a file I had cleverly labeled "Skinheads."

The media, nonetheless, began referring to me as an expert: "Officer Loren Christensen, the Portland Police Bureau's *expert* on white supremacy, blah, blah, blah." One newspaper in Chicago read, "Loren Christensen, a *national* expert on neo-Nazis . . ." It didn't take me long to realize that if they were going to call me an expert, I had better learn something about the subject. So I immediately began a crash course in white supremacy, reading everything I could find on racism, neo-Nazis, Hitler, and World War II. Except for a couple of magazine articles, there was nothing published about skinheads.

At the same time I was laboring toward the expertise I was already supposed to have, racist skinhead activity—vandalism, graffiti, harassment, intimidation, assault—was increasing. Although it was an unfortunate way to get an education, each new incident taught me more and more about the ugliness of the philosophy that drives the young Nazi skinheads. Then, in late 1988, all of Portland got a crash course in racist violence. Three racist skinheads brutally attacked three Ethiopians, beating one of them to death with a baseball bat. (See pages 9-10 for details.)

Portland Police homicide detectives Tom Nelson and Mike Hefley contacted me the next day to see what I had on skinheads, but since I was just starting to gather information, my files and my knowledge were minimal. In spite of this, however, Nelson and Hefley, who are real experts at catching killers, worked literally around the clock for a week until they had all the suspects in custody.

Once it was announced publicly that racist, neo-Nazi skinheads had been apprehended and charged with the unprovoked, racially motivated beating death of the black man, the local, national, and international media went ballistic. It was not uncommon for me to give six or seven interviews—radio, TV, newspapers, and magazines—during one workday. They would be waiting "on hold" when I arrived in the morning, and the phones would still be ringing when I left in the afternoon.

Since my name was mentioned in the stories, I was the person citizens called to voice their anger and fear. People phoned from other parts of the country wanting to know if their relatives were safe living in Portland. People of color who were considering moving to Portland called from New York, Oklahoma, and Florida worried that they would be killed by roving bands of neo-Nazis if they came.

This was an extremely stressful time of trying to learn about all the elements that form the white supremacy/skinhead philosophy, as well as trying not to make the police bureau or myself look foolish in the media. On top of that, I still had several other duties as a crime analyst in my precinct.

At that time, all of the gangs had become so violent throughout the city that it necessitated a specialized unit consisting of officers who did nothing else but work the rapidly increasing gang problem. The Gang Enforcement Team (GET) was created. The unit consisted of Portland Police officers, who made up its majority, along with officers on loan from surrounding jurisdictions, including the Oregon State Police, the Bureau of Alcohol, Tobacco and Firearms (AFT), and the Internal Revenue Service (IRS).

The State Police placed officers into GET to work skinheads, but because the distance between the gang office and my precinct was considerable, our working arrangement was somewhat awkward. To put all gang enforcement efforts under one roof, I was eventually transferred into GET in 1989 to work skinhead street gangs full time for the Portland Police Bureau and form a partnership with State Police Detective Griff Holland.

The text that follows contains information that we have garnered over the years working with racist and antiracist skinheads gangs. Some of our education came easily, and some of it came via the school of hard knocks. It's my hope that the compiled infor-

mation and tips will accelerate your learning of how to work skinhead gangs, and thus save you mistakes and wasted time. Skinheads, or any gang members for that matter, thrive in situations where the police and the public lack knowledge as to what they are seeing. Knowledge is power.

The issue of racist and antiracist skinhead gangs is a complex one. Just when you think you have it figured out, something new will come along to shoot down your perceived truth. For example, we had a white male gangster who was an active member in the black gang known as Bloods. He hung out with them, drank with them, and was even involved in a drive-by shooting against a Crip. A few months later, we documented him as a white supremacist because he was running with neo-Nazi skinheads and had formed a right-wing organization known as the National Socialist Front. Even in that capacity, he continued to communicate with individuals associated with the Blood gang.

To add more confusion to the pot, antiracist skinheads frequently change sides and become racist skins for a while, then switch back to become antiracist. One racist skinhead who had switched back and forth several times told us he was also bisexual. Does that make him bi-gangual as well?

One of the hardest of the hard-core racist skinheads, who we were convinced would die behind his beliefs, did a turnabout and now talks to school kids about the evils of racism.

One white supremacist leader, with neo-Nazi, Ku Klux Klan, and racist skinhead associates, and who has encouraged violence against blacks and other minorities in his speeches and publications, has worked with black racial activists to help black people.

For sure, there is nothing absolute in the business of skinhead gangs. In rewriting this text, I found I had used a large number of qualifying adjectives, such as *most*, *some*, and *many*, to describe how skinheads think and act. Thinking I had used them too often, I tried to delete many of them, but I could not. To remove them would have made the sentences inaccurate. One simply cannot make blanket statements about skinheads. It cannot be said that all skinheads think and act in the same way, because they do not. Just as all cops do not think and act the same way.

Significant anecdotes, examples, and quotes that should stand out have been set off by indentations. Although Portland's experience with skinheads could have supplied all of these excerpts, a sampling was used from across the country to show that white supremacy and skinhead gangs are a problem in every part of the United States.

Although this text is about street-level skinheads, it was necessary to include basic information about upper-echelon hate organizations, such as the Posse Comitatus, various racially conscious churches, and, of course, the Ku Klux Klan. These and other mentioned organizations have a tremendous influence on the young, impressionable skinheads. In turn, you will discover that skinheads have had a revitalizing effect on these once tired organizations.

A chapter has been included on skinhead activity in Europe. We cannot examine the skinhead issue in our country without looking at what is happening in

Germany, Hungary, and other countries. There are literally thousands upon thousands of neo-Nazi skinheads there fighting against immigration, homosexuals, and the handicapped. It's important for us to monitor their situation because our skinheads are definitely watching and learning from what is going on there. Some are even traveling to Europe to get firsthand experience from the heartland where Nazism and racism are once again gaining a foothold.

It was also important to include a chapter with a model plan for law enforcement agencies to use when they find themselves in the position of having to police a rally or a march by white supremacists of any ilk. It's a basic model that attempts to touch all the necessary bases when dealing with not only the white supremacists, but also with the counterdemonstrators who, more times than not, cause most of the problems.

The book begins by taking a quick look at how the problem began in one city, mine. I can speak best about Portland's situation because Griff Holland and I lived it, and when we look back over the years, we can see places where we could have done things differently and certainly better. Other cities have had an experience similar to Portland's, and it's guaranteed that there are unaffected cities where it's only a matter of time until it's their turn. Examining how it began in Portland, a city the Anti-Defamation League once called "the skinhead capital of the United States," will hopefully be of help to police agencies that are just starting to see the problem in their cities.

Racism, violence, and gang warfare are ugly, but these things exist together in our country today—and they aren't going away. Germans stood by in the 1930s and allowed these things to take root. We cannot let it happen here. In spite of the liberal press, right-wing manipulation of the law, a court system that seems to be upside down, and insufficient police funds, we must combat skinhead gangs with every means we have.

CHAPTER 1

During the mid-1980s, skinheads were mostly a part of the punk rock scene in Portland, Oregon. They were an odd-looking lot with their shaved heads and boots, but they caused no more problems than any of the other street kids.

Then in 1986, a skinhead by the street name Basher stabbed a white man to death behind a teen club in a violent end to a drug deal that had soured somehow. Although it was just another murder over drugs, it was the brutality of the incident that made the police wonder if there was more to these kids than just the freaky fashion statement they liked to present. Witnesses reported that Basher first plunged the knife into the man's groin, then sliced upward to his neck. He then turned to the cheering crowd of punker types and ceremoniously licked the dripping blade.

It was not until the summer of 1987 that skinheads began to act out racially. A large brawl at a teen club was one of the first indications they were something more than just goofy-looking kids who dressed funny and jerked their bald heads about to irritating music. The incident began when a few skinheads were kicked out of the club after they had confronted several blacks they thought were trying to pimp white girls. Enraged at being kicked

HOW SKINHEADS GOT STARTED IN ONE TOWN

out, the skins left, returning later with two dozen more boot-wearing shaved heads. The police arrived with two dozen of their own, and the fight was on. When it was over, police had arrested several skinheads and seized an assortment of crude weapons.

It appeared that when we were not looking, skinheads had developed a philosophy behind their exterior, an ugly philosophy that was especially dangerous when combined with their military appearance, their increasing numbers, and their growing propensity for explosive violence.

A few months later, in early 1988, three skinheads beat a Chinese man to the sidewalk, kicking him over and over while his wife and children watched in terror from inside their car. The press jumped on the incident's racial angle and, for several days, ran stories on the history and philosophy of racist skinheads and the ramifications of the unprovoked racial attack on the victim and his wife and children.

For the next several months, the police and the press monitored the activity of racist skinheads. Although the number of skinhead-perpetrated incidents throughout the summer and early fall amounted to no more than five or six a month and were relatively minor in nature, certain elements were slowly building and falling into place for bigger things to come.

Two groups had formed: POWAR, Preservation of the White Aryan Race, and ESWP, East Side White Pride. POWAR was primarily a downtown gang and ESWP was an east-side suburban gang. The gang structure gave the individuals, who were all new at being skinheads, a unity in which they were able to learn about white supremacy, party with people who had the same philosophy, move about town in force, and act out with strength in numbers.

Although antiracist skinheads had yet to emerge on the scene, there were many people who were nonracist skinheads, apolitical individuals who wore the regalia just as a fashion statement and as a way of identifying with a certain type of music. They were angry over the new, racist skins, especially the way in which the press portrayed all skinheads as being white supremacists. A few months later, tired of the hateful and fearful looks from the public, and for their own safety, the apolitical skinheads moved on to a different look, leaving only the racist skinheads sporting the boots, flight jackets, and clean-shaven heads.

In the early fall of 1988, a skinhead by the name of Dave Mazella came to Portland from California. Mazella was famous for having done the talk show circuit with Tom Metzger, the leader of WAR, White Aryan Resistance. Mazella also claimed to be vice president of Aryan Youth Movement (AYM), a branch of WAR. Because of his impressive credentials, the local skins looked up to him, listening carefully to what he taught them about the ways the big boys did things in California. Two years later, in court, Mazella claimed to have committed more than 80 assaults during his brief stay in Portland. The crimes, he said, were committed to teach the locals—skinheads and their victims—what being a true white warrior was all about.

Then on November 13, 1988, a cold, wet, Saturday night, Mazella's influence would manifest itself in bloodshed on a quiet residential street in southeast Portland. A car containing three Ethiopians stopped in front of an apartment complex to drop off a 27-year-old man by the name of Mulugetta Seraw. As the Ethiopians said their good-byes in the car, another car containing three men and three women pulled directly in front of them. The six occupants were skinheads, members of ESWP. All of them had had contact with Dave Mazella.

The confrontation began with racial slurs from the skinheads then moved quickly to a physical attack by the male skins. One of the Ethiopians fled, another crawled under a parked car, but the third, Mulugetta Seraw, was unable to escape. While two of the skinheads punched and kicked Seraw, the third, a thickly built skinhead known as Ken Death, ran to the car, retrieved a baseball bat, then ran back to the fight.

He cocked the bat high over his shoulder, as the girls cheered and shouted encouragement from the car. He swung it full force into the back of Seraw's head. Standing over the fallen man, Ken Death cocked the bat again and smashed it down onto Seraw's head. Then he did it again and again, like a wood chopper gone berserk. Next came the boot party, a ritual where skinheads stomp a downed person to oblivion. Mulugetta Seraw died a short time later.

Within a week, the skinheads were in jail, and the city was in turmoil. The story was in the headlines for days. Television, radio, and newspaper reporters called or descended from as far away as Germany, Japan, and Australia. Citizens held massive community meetings, marches, and rallies. Everyone wanted to know what had happened, how it could happen, and what was going to happen next.

While the city tried to make sense of it, word went out on the white supremacy grapevine that Portland was a mecca for skinheads. During the next few months, the number of skinhead-related crimes increased from five a month to more than 40. Although the arrests of the three skinheads literally dissolved the ESWP gang, they were quickly replaced by a half-dozen other gangs; the numbers of skinheads in the Portland area increased from 50 to more than 300.

Although the three killer skinheads subsequently pleaded guilty and were sentenced from nine years to life, activity did not stop or even decrease as it had in other cities where skinhead violence had taken place. Instead, more intimidation, more violence, and more death erupted. In 1990, antiracist skinheads came on the scene, adding a new element to the violence. The two philosophically different factions were instant rivals, which resulted in drive-by shootings, knifings, and bloody street brawls. In September 1990, Tom and John Metzger came to Portland to face Morris Dees of the Southern Poverty Law Center of Alabama in civil court. Dees, who was suing the Metzgers on behalf of Mulugetta

Seraw's family, is a formidable attorney who often champions the victims of bigotry, and some of his court cases have been made into television movies. With an unprecedented police presence, the two-week civil trial concluded with the jury finding the Metzgers responsible for sending agents to Portland to encourage skinhead violence. When the gavel landed, Tom Metzger and his son John were $12,500,000 in debt.

Since the Metzger trial, activity has been erratic, sometimes up, sometimes down. Although aggressive, proactive police work has decreased the number of incidents and skinheads, periodic violence continues to flare. The presence of skinheads in the City of Roses is still a concern to Portlanders, as well it should be. The skinheads show no sign of going away.

CHAPTER 2

So that we are all thinking the same thing when the word gang is used in this text, let us define it as follows. A gang does the following:

- Conspires to commit, or commits, crimes against individuals or groups based on color, race, religion, sexual preference, national origin, or against rival gang associations
- Uses a name or common identifying sign or symbol, or has an identifiable leadership
- Has a high rate of interaction among members to the exclusion of other groups
- Claims a neighborhood and/or geographical territory
- Wears distinctive types of clothing, exhibits distinctive appearance, or communicates in a peculiar or unique style

WHY DO YOUNG PEOPLE BECOME SKINHEADS?

A person becomes a skinhead for many of the same reasons young people join other gangs. Some join because of the excitement of gang activity, peer pressure, attention, respect, strength, sense of family, and survival. It's exciting to be in a skinhead gang. There are always beer parties, slam dances, rallies, and fights.

WHO ARE THE SKINHEADS?

> When one racist skinhead woman left her wealthy family to become involved in the white supremacy movement, she gave up fancy cars, European vacations , and private schools to live the more exhilarating life style of a neo-Nazi skinhead: shooting assault rifles, fighting in the streets, and demonstrating in public places against the Zionist Occupational Government.

Some get involved in a skinhead gang because of peer pressure. Some find it hard not to be involved when all their friends are doing it. A follower may be led into the philosophy and the gang before he realizes what he is getting into. Then, after he is in, it's difficult to get out.

Skinheads get a lot of attention from other young people, old people, minorities, the media, and the police. A skinhead may come from a family environment where he was ignored or treated as if he was a bother. But when he is in a gang with his head shaved, wearing a flight jacket and big boots, people notice him. It may be the first time he has gotten attention, and it feels good; he perceives it as something positive.

Along with the attention comes a sort of respect. As he stomps down the sidewalk with other skins, people fold out of the way. They will point at him; some people look scared. Other kids in school will talk about him and leave him alone. Although most people would see this as negative, a new skinhead, a kid who has been living without a sense of self-value, will see this attention as positive. He is suddenly someone special; he is finally getting respect.

> One skinhead said he used to identify with the punks, who projected an air of toughness. "But the skinheads are tougher," he insists. "No one fights with the skinheads. So I got in with them."

An individual skinhead becomes strong within a gang, because as a member he sees everything as "us against them." It's rare for a skinhead to act out by himself. In Portland, there has never been an assault committed by one skinhead acting alone. All have been done by at least two and as many as 35.

Some skinheads get a sense of family from the gang. Their family circumstances are usually such that they don't fulfill their needs. Although what the gang really offers is negative, they don't see it that way. The gang structure gives them the family they want, or at least a sense of it.

Skinheads often get angry at the media, accusing them of putting skinheads into a neat package of goose-stepping zealots, or of creating an easy psychology that explains their actions.

> "They say we all come from broken homes, and that is why we became skinheads," one skinhead female complained. "That's partially true. Not that we didn't have these racist feelings beforehand, but now we belong to something. We do have family. It's almost like saying we're white trash. We're all from poor families. We all had such sad childhoods that we decided to get together and beat people up."
>
> "To see us just as a street gang makes us seem less dangerous," warned one skinhead leader.

Skinheads often refer to their skinhead gang members as family.

A white person may join a skinhead gang for survival, especially if he is in a situation where there is a large population of minorities and where there are other gangs. Many skins will say they became interested in white supremacy and ultimately a racist gang because they felt it was necessary to survive in a juvenile detention facility, in high school, while hanging out in their neighborhood, or while living on the street.

It often seems the only thing some racist skinheads have going for them is their white skin. Their self-esteem comes from associating with other racist skinheads who continually give them recognition and pats on the back for having been born Caucasian. Their belief is that they are white and heterosexual, so therefore they are superior.

In some cases, a young person will take up racism as an act of rebellion. Equal rights and civil rights are conventional doctrine in our society—that is, politically correct in our schools, churches, media, and other public and social institutions. So rebelling against this conventionality, what used to be called the establishment, is a way to be defiant. And, of course, defiance is what being a teenager is all about. Whether their adoption of this philosophy is permanent and whether it leads them into violent acts depend on their peers and to what degree they buy into the "education" they get while involved in the white supremacy movement.

The antiracist skinhead becomes involved in a gang for all the same psychological and sociological reasons as the racist skinhead. While they have a different philosophy and political stance, the individuals who form the different skinhead factions have the same basic needs and wants.

As we shall see later, with some skinheads the ideology of the gang is not as important as being a member of it. Initially, they never give the philosophy a passing thought. They simply join because their friends are in it or because they are attracted to all that the gang offers. Once they are in and begin to learn what it's all about, they might take on the beliefs of its members. Then again, they might just continue for the ride, with little care about the gang's philosophical underpinnings.

A prime example of the person who joins a gang to fulfill the needs listed above is the person who straddles the fence. He will belong to a racist skinhead gang for a while, then switch over and become an antiracist, then later switch back again. This is a person who likes and needs the gang structure, and although he may put on a good outward appearance, he could care less about the gang's philosophy.

INVENTING THEIR SUBCULTURE

Being any kind of gang member means you have the power to invent your own subculture. Many gangs continually change what they are about. One week their reason for existence is to keep the park clear of another gang they deem unfit to be in it. The next week, however, they have forgotten about the park because they have become actively involved in the drug world.

Racist skinheads have created a subculture of people whose purpose is to act as soldiers assigned the task of cleaning America of unwanted elements, and they even have the power to decide which elements. They have been taught by the upper-echelon white supremacist organizations that the white culture is on the decline, a result of minorities having large families and whites being manipulated by the Jewish-controlled government to abort their children. They have been brainwashed to believe the white working man is duty-bound to fight to return America to the white men who built it.

Antiracists claim to be the true skinheads and will fight to restore honor to what they see as the legitimate skinhead subculture.

POWER

The concept of power is very important to skinhead gang members. It's what they are about, and in most

cases, it's what they lacked before they became involved
in the gangs. To people who get their sense of power in
more positive and constructive ways, it may be hard to
relate to the psychological high a skinhead gang member
feels as he stomps about with four or five other skins. To
try to understand, let's look at some areas where skinheads, both racist and antiracist, obtain a sense of power.

- *They have a perception and reputation of being tough.*
  Skinheads absolutely love the image they project.
  Their appearance—military-style boots, military flight
  jacket, camouflage pants, shaved head, tattoos—sends
  out a message to the world that they are warriors,
  ready and willing to fight. They feel strongest when
  they are dressed up in their regalia, standing on a
  street corner, sucking hard on cigarette after cigarette,
  glaring menacingly at passersby.
- *They derive power from their numbers.* Alone they are
  nothing. Together, two, three, twenty strong, they are
  fearless, undaunted. They see themselves as a mighty
  force ready and more than eager to kick butt.
- *They get power from being white.* Their white skin is the
  only thing some skinheads have going for them. They
  may be poor, uneducated, and disenfranchised, but at
  least they have their prized pigmentation. This gives
  them a feeling of power over people of color, whom they
  see as inferior to them. Skinhead gatherings are often a
  time to celebrate their whiteness, basking in its glory
  while they disparage all people of color.
- *They receive power from their sense of racial superiori-
  ty.* This is closely tied to being white, but goes a step
  further to embrace the entire nation of Caucasian people. Since the other races are considered nonentities,
  racist skinheads, especially those who follow the
  teachings of the Christian Identity church, believe the
  white race is superior because it's the only race that
  God gave his spirit to.
- *Their "us against them" mentality gives them power.*
  It can get lonely being right, when a person believes

Two skinheads confront a black man.

only he is right and everyone else is wrong. But when
he is with others who believe the same way as he
does, he feels stronger and more confident that his
belief is a valid one. On top of that, when his belief is
dramatically different from the norm, a perception
develops of "us against them." This creates cohesiveness within the gang and a strong feeling of power,
especially when members have a sense of righteousness about the belief and the knowledge that others
will stand with them to defend it.

- *They obtain power from their goals.* A skinhead gang's
goals can be as simple as "let's beat up a queer" or as
involved as joining forces with a more established
organization to establish an all-white territory in the
United States. It's working together toward a common
objective that gives the gang its sense of power.

THE VIOLENT GANG

Although all skinhead gangs commit crimes, some
gangs are more violent than others. The violent gangs

spend much of their time gathering weapons, planning and carrying out violent acts. Membership in the gang will consist of some hard-core skinheads who truly believe in the rightness of what they are doing and some less than hard-core individuals who only use the skinhead concept as an excuse to do violence.

The leaders, when they exist, tend to be charismatic and have an innate need to lead and control others, although controlling a skinhead gang is almost impossible. Leaders and followers almost always overestimate their importance, their numbers, and the power their group can wield. This inflated sense of importance has always existed with white supremacists, even as far back as the early days of the Ku Klux Klan.

With the violent gang, there is generally more fighting within the ranks and against other skinhead factions than there is against the hated Jewish-controlled government. A friend or ally one day will be an enemy the next. Allegiance to the gang is often weak; a skinhead who claims to be one of Hitler's Boots one week will belong to the West Side Oi Boyz the next.

If there is anything positive to say about the violent gangs, it's that they don't last long. Since they are out committing crimes of assault, arson, rape, and murder, they get the attention of the police much faster than the skinhead gang that simply writes graffiti on walls.

> In New York City, a clash between punk rockers and skinheads left one punk rocker dead and two others hospitalized with stab wounds. The victims were stabbed by Hispanic and black right-wing skinheads as they tried to help a punk rocker band member who was under attack by neo-Nazi skinheads.
>
> •
>
> One skinhead gang went on a weekend rampage. They attacked people with two-by-fours, fought in the streets with each other, smashed windows out of an old woman's house with a bat, threw Molotov cocktails at each other, and deliberately rammed parked cars with their cars.

Three days later, every participant was in jail, which resulted in the demise of the gang.

•

A 19-year-old skinhead in Denver, Colorado, decided he "just wanted to shoot somebody, not just one guy, a whole street. It just makes me feel good." The skinhead approached a man in an alley and decided to steal his car. He shot the man twice in the head as he begged for his life. Then the skinhead set the car ablaze with the victim in it. Two days later he held the police at bay with a gun pointed at a friend's head.

The cohesiveness of the violent gang makes them powerful and dangerous to law enforcement. They see the police as the enemy, Zionist Occupational Government's (ZOG) muscle. Skinheads and all white supremacists live in a fantasy world where great battles take place between white warriors and the despised ZOG police. It's important to keep in mind that given the less than stable mental state of some skinheads, often only a thin line exists between fantasy and reality.

HOW MANY SKINHEADS ARE THERE?

Reporters, students, cops, and citizens always want to know how many racist skinheads there are. That's an impossible question to answer because you can't count them. They don't register anywhere or call the police and provide them with the size of their gang. You can't sit on a rooftop and count them as they pass below because not all skinheads look like what you might imagine.

Even sophisticated monitoring organizations—such as the Klanwatch Project of the Southern Poverty Law Center in Montgomery, Alabama, the Center for Democratic Renewal in Atlanta, or the Anti-Defamation League—cannot provide an accurate count of skinheads or any of the various organized white supremacy factions.

Some rough numbers can be thrown out for consideration. Likely, they err on the conservative side. The monitoring organizations estimate that between 10,000 and 20,000 members belong to white supremacy organizations nationally, with at least 10 passive supporters for every one member. Quick math brings the total of skinheads/sympathizers to 200,000—and, again, this is a conservative guesstimate.

Many white supremacists belong to more than one organization. For example, skinheads who belong to The Boot Kickers may also hang out with another gang of skins. Some skinheads associate with Ku Klux Klan organizations. Some neo-Nazi skins attend gatherings with followers of the Nazi philosophy who are not young skinheads, but adults. Some skins attend a Christian Identity church where the majority of the congregation are hardworking, middle-aged people dressed in normal clothing.

Maybe we can use the number of subscribers to such right-wing newspapers as Tom Metzger's California-based WAR newspaper or the Liberty Lobby's Washington, D.C.-based, *The Spotlight*. WAR has claimed 30,000 subscribers and *The Spotlight* 100,000. Consider, however, that there are many organizations and gangs that subscribe to only one paper, but dozens of members who read it. Therefore, subscription numbers only reflect how many papers are sold, not how many people read them, sympathize with the views expressed, and work for what the papers advocate.

If a police department has a criterion for documenting people as gang members in their police computers, the number will never reflect the true number of skinheads out on the streets. For every one skinhead who is documented as a gangster, there are two or three others who have not yet come to the attention of the police, so are not in the system.

The number of hate crimes does not correspond to the number of skinheads or white supremacists in a city, state, or the country. Besides, most hate crimes are not committed by members of an organized group or gang anyway. Of course the very presence of a neo-Nazi skinhead gang in a city, and the publicity it generates, may allow some so-called straight people to come out of the closet with their racist feelings and act out on them.

As you can see, coming up with a valid number is virtually impossible. We can safely say there are thousands of people who claim membership to white supremacy organizations and thousands more who sympathize with the cause but do not belong to an organization. We know from gathering information from police departments around the country that skinheads, individuals who actually dress up in the clothing and shave their heads, number in the thousands. We also know from the same sources that skinhead gangs have members who dress in regular street clothes and run with those who dress in typical skinhead garb. They don't look like skinheads, but they act like them. Do we call them skinheads? Do we count them as such?

Determining a way to count skinheads is difficult, if not impossible. It's safe to say, however, that for every obvious white supremacist, there are many more who support and cheer on the cause from behind their closed doors, with their ballots in the voting booth, and with cash sent through the mail.

Antiracist skinheads are just as difficult to count, if not more so. Some skins who wear the skinhead regalia align themselves with antiracist organizations, which are made up primarily of people who do not dress like skinheads. Then when they act out together, say to violently oppose something, the tendency is to count them all as antiracist skinheads.

DESCRIPTION OF A SKINHEAD

Racist skinheads believe all whites are racists and that skinheads are just braver than most whites because they publicly exhibit their philosophy. They say their shaved heads, flight jackets, and boots show everyone what they believe. Antiracist skinheads, who look basically the same, take issue with racist skinheads' assertions that the boots, jackets, and shaved heads automatically depict a racist philosophy. Later we will examine the problems this creates in the form of intergang violence. But for now, let's look at the basic description of a racist and antiracist skinhead.

TYPICAL SKINHEAD

	Racist	*Antiracist*
AGE	13–23 years old	Same
RACE	White	Predominately white, but will also include blacks, Native Americans, Asians, and others
HAIR	*Males* will usually be bald or wear their hair short	Same
	Females occasionally will completely shave their heads, but usually wear it punk style: shaved in the front, long in the back, or vice versa, and frequently bleached blond	Same
CLOTHING	Green, gray, or black flight jacket	Same
	Blue jeans, black pants, or camouflage pants	Same
	Military-type boots or Doc Marten boots	Same
TATTOOS & PATCHES	Swastikas, "White Power," "Sieg Heil," "Skins," Confederate flag, KKK emblem	Swastika with a diagonal line through it, "Sharps," Sharp patch
VIOLENCE	Both groups have a strong propensity for violence	

This skinhead sports the classic regalia: Doc Marten boots, rolled-up jeans, flight jacket with patches, and shaved head.

Let's look at these descriptors more closely and examine the significance behind them.

Hair

Skinhead hair, or the lack of it, is oftentimes a confusing issue. The term skinhead has more or less been adopted by the media to mean any white supremacist street thug. As the name implies, the person should be bald-headed, but that is not always the case. Over the years, skinheads have alternatively shaved their heads or worn their hair an inch long or at times, at shoulder length. With the exception of the occasional skinhead with sideburns, they generally do not have facial hair. This applies to both racist and antiracist skins.

In the early days, virtually everyone claiming to be a racist skinhead had a shaved head. They were "shaved for battle" and proud of it. It served as a symbol of who and what they were, and it was used as a tool to intimidate. Admittedly, a shaved head can give a face a menacing look by accenting hard eyes and a strong neck. But on some skins, the absence of hair will make weak eyes appear weaker and a skinny neck scrawnier, especially if there is a large, protruding Adam's apple bobbing up and down.

Sometimes, a skinhead will only shave his head for special events, such as a rally or a demonstration. All other times, he will wear it short or medium length so as not to draw the attention of the police or turn off an employer. There are some skinheads who never shave their heads. They will wear a flight jacket, Doc Marten boots, and be covered with tattoos, but choose to keep their hair length normal or even longer than normal. Others keep their heads shaved all the time as part of their identity.

When a skinhead works for an employer who doesn't like the shaved head, he may simply wear a hat. It's not uncommon for an employer to be unaware he has a skin-head working for him, especially if the job is an outside one where a coat and hat are worn all the time.

From time to time, an edict will be dispensed from Aryan Nations or Tom Metzger for skinheads to grow out their hair. Usually, this comes after a major incident when there is a great deal of attention directed at them. When such an order comes down, some skinheads obey

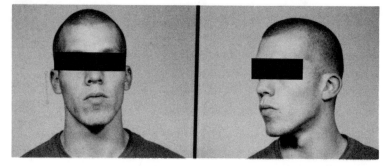

Skinhead is a bit of a misnomer since members wear a variety of hair styles.

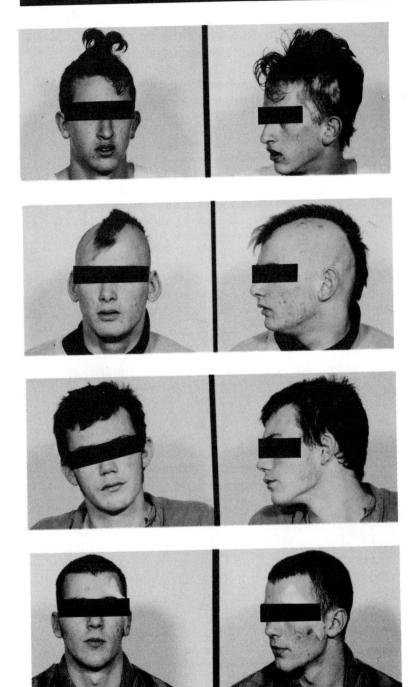

it, some don't. And even when they do grow it out, a few months later they usually shave it again.

> After skinheads brutally beat a black man to death, word went out among the city's skinheads to grow out their hair to prevent the police from identifying them so easily. Longer hair and an overall conservative dress also made them less of a target of enraged straight citizens and black gangs.

●

> Months before his civil suit in Portland, Oregon, Tom Metzger told Portland skinheads to let their hair grow and to wear normal clothing. "Hanging out on a street corner in Portland is not my idea of working for the white race," he said. "You don't have to change your views . . . but why dress in a way or cut your hair in a way that every time you walk down the street you're either going to be thrown up against a wall by some overzealous cop or be attacked by some gang or some World War II veteran or something?"

Few females shave their heads completely bald, but when they do you can assume they are hard-core. Most females cut their hair in the style of a punk rocker. They may have a flattop with long bangs or a flattop with long hair in the back. It's not uncommon for them to bleach their hair, so as to emulate the true Aryan look, the look of the Viking princess.

Flight Jacket

The U.S. Air Force flight jacket is the most popular jacket worn by both racist and antiracist skinheads. It comes in green, black, and brown. Neo-Nazi skins prefer the black flight in some parts of the country, but generally skins wear whatever color they can get.

They like to adorn their jackets with patches, flags, and felt pen scribbling. The patches denote their affiliation or their desire to affiliate with various groups and organizations. For example, they might have patches of the Ku Klux Klan or Aryan Nations on their shoulders or over a breast pocket. They may wear a patch of the Confederate flag on one shoulder and, very commonly, the American flag on the other. After all, they believe in America—albeit an all-white one.

The flight jacket is so much a part of their philosophy that they even wear it on hot days. It's their warrior uniform, their chosen attire for battle.

Braces

Skinheads refer to suspenders as braces, a term favored by English skinheads. Some skinheads wear them all the time, some never do, and, just to confuse us, some wear them just once in a while. If the skin is an occasional wearer, he will usually put them on for a specific event, such as a concert or some kind of get-together. It's rather like a military person wearing all his ribbons, medals, citations, and decorative ropes for a special event. As a matter of routine, while skinheads are just hanging around on a corner, they may or may not wear braces.

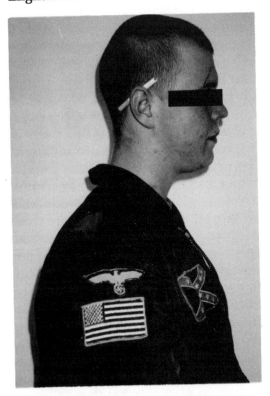

This skinhead's flight jacket is embellished with an American flag to show patriotism, a Confederate flag to show loyalty to the ways of the old South, and a swastika to show Nazi sympathies.

Some skinheads choose a specific color, while others wear whatever color they can get. Colors may have a different meaning in different parts of the state or country. Racist skins who believe in the significance of color often wear red or white braces. Red braces usually symbolize their blood, meaning they will shed it for "The Cause," everything they believe in and stand for. Sometimes red simply denotes that they are neo-Nazi skins. White braces represent the white race they are fighting for. Some skins wear black to signify that they are neutral, neither racist nor antiracist. There are not many neutral skins around anymore, since it is unsafe on the street to look like a skinhead and not have politics.

A popular expression in the early days of the skinhead movement defined how the braces were worn. They would say, "When our heads are shaved and our braces are down, we're ready to kick ass." If a skinhead wore his braces over his shoulders, it was somewhat safe to assume that he was going about his routine business. If several skinheads wore their braces down around their thighs, it meant they were out to cause mayhem.

Today, rules of proper braces etiquette may or may not be followed as strictly as in earlier times. There are some groups that wear them up all the time, while others consistently wear them down. There are some individuals who wear them simply because they like the style, not for any symbolic reasons. Some skins wear them down, even when they are not on a specific mission of mischief, while others commit vandalism and assault while wearing their braces up. Some skinheads never wear them at all.

The bottom line is that you cannot automatically assume anything about their braces, or lack of them, until you make contact with a specific skinhead or group of skins and ask. Even then, as always, what they tell you may or may not be true.

Trousers

Usually, skinheads wear tan dickies, military green or brown camouflage pants, black or blue jeans—although, as mentioned earlier, some skinheads refuse to wear Levi jeans because of the company's perceived Jewish connection.

Sometimes they roll the pant legs down over the boots, especially when they are at work or out by themselves and don't want to draw any attention to themselves. But when a group is completely dressed up and moving about in a pack, the pant legs will be rolled up or tucked in to expose the full glory of their Doc Marten boots.

Doc Marten Boots

Doctor Marten boots, usually called Doc Martens, Dockers, or Docs, are the boot of choice among skinheads. Those who don't know about or can't afford Doc Martens wear army boots or even old, beat-up work boots. But the coveted boot is the Doc Marten, the one exported from England and the one that identifies them as true skins. Steel-toed Doc Martens are preferred since they are better to kick with.

> One skinhead deliberately stuck the toe of his boot under the rolling wheel of a car with no effect on the boot or the ignoramus' foot.

There are three colors of Doc Martens to choose from: brown, ox-blood red, and black, with varying numbers of eyelets, the largest count in a boot that nearly reaches the knees. Although most of the time a skinhead will take whatever he can get, neo-Nazi skins usually choose black, but as with other parts of their clothing, colors symbolize different things in various areas of the country. There are no hard-and-fast rules about the color of the boots.

The laces are significant with some skinheads. As with the braces, red will denote neo-Nazism and/or the blood they are willing to shed for their fight. White denotes white power/white pride. Green laces often denote that the skin is a gay-basher. Some original, hard-core skins will never change laces. If one breaks, it will be repaired, not replaced. This is a tradition of sorts that goes back to their working-class roots.

Robbing, or "taxing," another for his boots is common. Two or more skins will see someone wearing Docs or a good-looking pair of military jump boots and decide to take them from him. If the person is unknown, the skins may ask him if he is "white pride." If he says no, and sometimes even if he says yes, the skins will knock him down and take his boots away from him.

> One large, muscular skinhead in Washington state was feared for his frequent taxing of boots from other skins. One night as he slept in his sleeping bag, four other skins, tired of his bullying, beat him to death with 2x4s.

Tattoos and Emblems

Racist skinheads, especially neo-Nazis, like to wear Nazi paraphernalia, such as jewelry depicting swastikas, German Iron Crosses, and double lightning bolts. These can be in the form of lapel pins; ear, nose, or finger rings; necklaces; or bracelets. Skins take great pride in owning legitimate pieces, real antiques they've picked up from collectors at gun shows.

Their tattoos are usually swastikas, Iron Crosses, "SS," skulls, Viking warriors, barbed wire, and words such as "Skins," "White Power," and "Nazi." No part of their bodies is immune to tattoos, including their faces and their shaved heads.

The February 1990 issue of the *Oklahoma Separatist*, a white supremacy newsletter, had this to say about tattooing:

> White Power tattoo designs are becoming the latest phenomena in the field of Racial Revolution. As the White Working Class awakes to their impending fate, White Backlash against alien oppressors is often manifested in White Blackwork [a style of tattooing]. The Skinhead movement and the tattoo enthusiasts associated with the society has become one of the most creative areas in the field of progressive tattooing. Whereas some folks

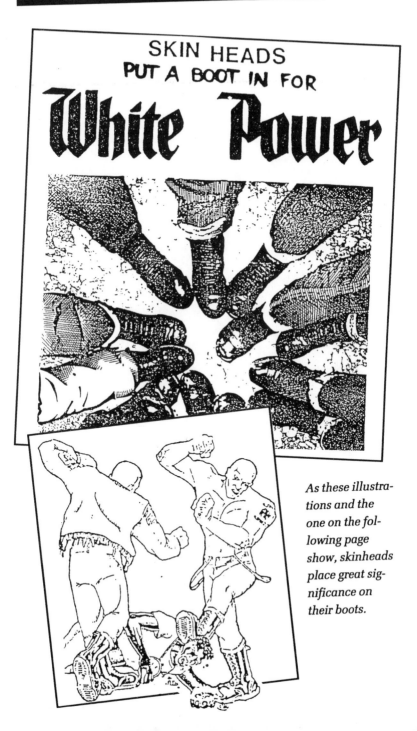

SKIN HEADS
PUT A BOOT IN FOR
White Power

As these illustrations and the one on the following page show, skinheads place great significance on their boots.

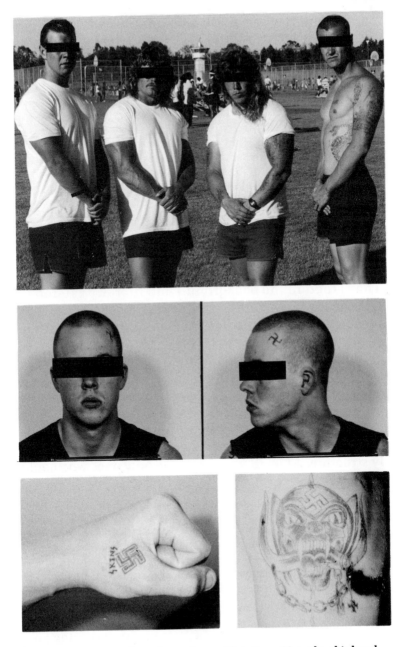

Skinheads love to adorn themselves with tattoos. Note the skinhead who tattooed a backward swastika on his forehead.

get their tattoos on inconspicuous or conventional segments of the body, Skinhead tattoos often appear on the face, hands and top of their head. Lately I've been seeing some brilliant and very beautiful pieces sported by guys and gals from every segment of the movement . . .

●

One particularly dense racist skinhead spent considerable time and pain tattooing a large swastika on his forehead. Although the lines were straight and the ink was rich, the swastika was tattooed into his flesh—backwards.

FEMALE SKINHEADS

When the skinhead phenomena began in the mid-1980s, the females appeared to be subservient to the men. They stood in the background and literally catered to their needs. They didn't speak unless spoken to and they never spoke to the media. Then around 1989 the situation began to change.

Fliers appeared on walls and telephone poles advising: "White Women Unite!" Apparently it suddenly occurred to the young skinhead women that the white race could not perpetuate itself without them. They began to realize they were significant players in the white supremacy movement and, in particular, the white family structure. After all, they were the only ones who could bring forth the coveted white Aryan babies.

> At age 42, Darlene is the Grand Secretary and wife of the Grand Dragon of the Georgia KKK. In that position she is a role model for women and a leader of men—i.e., women and men who follow white supremacy. As a proud grandmother, she says one of her happiest moments was when she heard her granddaughter's first word: "Nigger."

Aryan Women's League (AWL), founded in 1988 by a woman calling herself Monique Wolfgang, is an off-shoot of Tom Metzger's WAR. Metzger's daughter Lynn, a blond

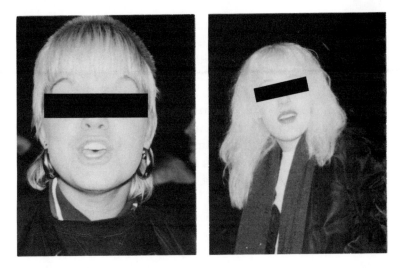

Female skinheads have taken a more active role in the movement in recent years.

woman in her early twenties and a senior member of AWL, says proudly, "We are definitely not feminists. We work with our men totally."

Tabitha would agree.

Tabitha is a 22-year-old woman who fervently believes that women should stay in the home and support their men. She believes men deserve a woman who tends to her man's needs and desires first, rather than being concerned about a big board meeting the next day at her office.

When she was asked if she was aware which decade she was in, she exploded, "I know very well that these are the '90s. But I also know that the reason there is so much unemployment in the United States and there are so many problems with youth is because there are so many white mothers in the work force. If white women would stay home and raise their children and support their men, the white children would be better off and there would be more jobs available for the white working man." Tabitha wants six children, and she has already selected their German names.

Many skinhead women, and even some of the men, have a fantasy image of the way America used to be before the "mud races" became so prominent. They have images of powerfully built men, their muscles straining as they smashed rocks with huge hammers, their bodies sweating under a blazing sun. Indeed, their art, posters, and fliers depict this image, accompanied with bold print proclaiming: "White Men Built This Country."

The AWL appears to be a loose network of several hundred women living in several states and several countries, including Canada, where Women for Aryan Unity is based. It conducts baby-clothes drives and raises money by various methods for "political prisoners," white supremacists currently serving time in prison. Their literature talks about the need to educate themselves in first aid, self-defense, and gardening. They express concern about the preservation of the environment and wildlife.

The husband of the founder wrote a letter in support of AWL that leaves little doubt about the organization's objectives:

> The AWL isn't some Jew dyke/we hate white males type of deal. AWL is trying to battle the Jew/mud/zombie/mutant degenerate lesbos. Any man who feels threatened might as well hang it up because he is no man at all, let alone a White Warrior!!

Women of the AWL agree. "The feminist movement was started by a Jewish woman to get women into the I-hate-men era," asserts Lynn Metzger. "It was a conspiracy to take women out of the home and lower the white birth rate." All white supremacists believe that abortion is a Jewish conspiracy to reduce the white birth rate. "We have no concern for the other races," Metzger says.

A female skinhead who has an abortion is immediately ostracized. Killing an unborn white child does not coincide with love of the white race. A female skin cannot have it both ways.

Many skinhead mothers and pregnant women choose to take on a more conservative appearance. They may wear their Doc Marten boots and a nice sweater, or a flight jacket and Reebok shoes. Their hair is generally conservative. "It's a way of protecting ourselves and our children," says one female skinhead. "I can be more protective of my child if I can't be singled out because of my appearance. Babies are more important than my hair. They are the future of the white race."

These skins disdain females who are not true white supremacists, but rather groupies or "rich bitches" who hang around their men for the excitement. They refer to them as "abortion queens" and "sluts." They get angry at their men who say one thing but succumb to such females when the opportunity arises.

Females become skinheads for the same varied reasons as males. Some get involved for no other reason than wanting to be with a boyfriend who is in the gang. Others have had negative experiences while they were growing up that led to a racist philosophy. Some have attended schools where they had bad experiences with minorities. Others say their racist philosophy is a self-defense against what they see going on in the United States. Some of the young women learned racism from their parents.

> Jane grew up in a family where all of the men were hard working welders, construction workers, and carpenters. Nightly she would hear their complaints. "The niggers are getting all the best jobs, all the advancement. The goddamn spics are taking our jobs and the food off our table." She listened to this daily, beginning as a toddler and continuing into her teens. Her opinions entrenched by the time she was 16 and met a group of skinheads. Today she is teaching her child the same things she was taught.
>
> •
>
> "In second grade there was only me and one other white kid," says Terri, a hard-core skinhead girl. "All the rest were Mexicans. It made me feel

> uncomfortable. I didn't have any friends, I didn't want any friends. One thing I noticed, though, was the difference in intelligence between the races. The Mexican kids couldn't spell anything, words like 'what' and 'when.'"

Girls with experiences such as Terri's and Jane's find comfort when they meet racist skinheads for the first time. Feelings they have held in for years can now be expressed freely among those who share the same beliefs. Being with others who feel the same gives them a sense of security, a sense of belonging, and a new sense of power.

> "When I joined with the skins and shaved my hair, I felt powerful," says Vicky. "I was only 14 years old, but I had a solid identity. I was a skin. I felt really confident, ready for anything. I felt above everybody. That's the feeling you have when you're shaved. You're ready to fight for what you believe in. There's no turning back."

> •

> "Skinhead women are tough," says Tom Metzger. "I once saw one beat up a man."

As skinhead women take a more active role alongside the men in their fight for white supremacy, they are finding themselves involved in serious crimes. Such as:

- Beating a skinhead in Florida who was discovered to be Jewish
- Attacking several minorities in Tulsa, Oklahoma
- Vandalizing a synagogue in Tennessee
- Striking a man with a steel pipe in Portland, Oregon
- Pummeling a fellow skinhead to death in Vancouver, Washington
- Cheering and encouraging male skins as they beat a black man to death in Oregon
- Murdering a black man in Reno, Nevada
- Assaulting an Iranian couple in California

A group of female skinheads snap out the Nazi arm salute.

One male skinhead said this about his wife:

> "This woman has strode beside myself and other warriors into full impact combat, proving herself in more ways than one. White, racially-conscious women are most beautiful when they are in battle."

Women are also becoming leaders in the movement. This can be seen in the old groups, such as the KKK, as well as with the skinheads. Every so often a woman comes into the organization who has the brains, the leadership skills, and the desire to go to the top, but it's not an easy path for the woman to take. Along the way she is going to confront many obstacles in the form of macho males who will take issue with her lofty position. Some have already taken the road and survived the obstacles. You can count on more to come.

Today, the skinhead woman knows her place in the world of white supremacy. She may still believe her man is boss and her role is to support him and raise good

Aryan children, but she is more aware now than ever before that her role is a significant one. She knows her man needs her and her race needs her Aryan children.

MUSIC

You have not lived until you have been to a skinhead slam dance. The hard-driving, thumping, screaming, banging, thundering explosion of the most god-awful sounds this side of hell can only remotely fit the definition of music. It pile-drives into the souls of the young skinheads and seems to propel them into a mad frenzy of violence.

Slam dancing, as the name implies, involves the purposeful smashing of bodies together. With smiles on their faces, they bang shoulders, chests, and heads and throw wild punches, often not really caring who gets hit, as long as they feel the orgasmic pleasure of flesh smashing against flesh. Injuries are commonplace and ambulances do a brisk business. It's an agreeable riot that almost always ends amiably in spite of the many fights spawned during the dancing.

But there is more to the music than just the primitive rage it arouses. There is also the message. The lyrics tell the skinheads they are heroic warriors fighting for the white race, fighting for all that belongs to them.

Skinhead music serves two functions: it arouses the requisite rage in these angry young skins, and it reinforces the message of racial and religious discrimination.

A handmade flag glorifying skinheads and their "oi" music was found on the wall in a juvenile detention center.

Through the medium of music, their brains are bombarded repetitively with racial and religious prejudice. It is a simple, primal tool used to advance their message, to themselves and to all those who have not yet heard it.

They call the music white power or sometimes "oi" music. A Cockney phrase, oi means "hey" and is used as a greeting and an expression of unity among some racial skinheads. The music is heavier than heavy metal, and as skins say, "It's music to riot by." When skinheads gather at each other's apartments or in parks, music is an essential part of the ambiance. It celebrates who they are, what they believe in, and what they want. Much of the music advocates nazism, racism, violence, and even genocide. It's enticing to some teens teetering on the brink of being a racist skinhead, and it entrenches those who already are.

Skinhead festivals, usually in the summer, occur for any number of reasons. The setting is often rural, usually on a supporter's farm, so the revelers can party freely in the open air. Bandstands are adorned with rebel flags and banners depicting boldly colored swastikas. Most of the musicians can barely play their instruments, but that is not important; they are not trying to get the listeners to hum along.

As the music roars, the skins snap out stiff-armed

salutes, shout "Sieg Heil!" and "White power," guzzle beer, and dance about the bandstand like ancient tribesmen around a bonfire. One skinhead described his music this way:

> "The music of the skinhead is a most powerful, hard-driving style of rock and roll we call Oi. It is nothing like punk rock, hard-core, or heavy metal. Oi stands alone in classification with its crisp beat and melodic tune variations. The system has tried to steal our music and destroy it. Both attacks have failed. Oi is for warriors and the lyrics of most Oi bands sing proud racial statements with powerful words to oppose the enemy."

In the late 1980s, WAR leader Tom Metzger realized that music was the fastest and most effective way to get his message of white supremacy across to young people. He knew, as other movements have known, that music has a special power to stir emotions, especially in the young, and it's an excellent way to teach bigotry. Certainly, it's easier and more enjoyable than having to listen to a lecture. In an article in his WAR newspaper Metzger said, "Music is one of the greatest propaganda tools around. You can influence more people with a song than you can a speech."

The killer of Mulegetta Seraw in Portland, Oregon, was a member of a "death metal" band. As a musician, he called himself Ken Death and said he preferred metal bands such as Mega Death and Slayer. (See his lyrics at the end of this section.)

Two infamous skinheads told police this about white power music:

> "It motivates you and it really makes a lot of sense . . .
>
> •
>
> "Music is number one. It's the best way to reach people. Through music, people can start getting into the scene, then you can start educating them. Politics through music."

In the Beginning

The white power music of today began in the "hard-rocker" culture of mid-1960s England. At that time, working-class youths were looking for a different sound than that of the hippies and the mods. Although they had long hair as opposed to shaved heads, they wore boots and braces like today's skins and frequented reggae clubs. They soon developed a tough reputation because of their frequent fights with the police, soccer players, homosexuals, and hippies. They began shaving their heads to prevent getting their hair pulled, as well as to look different from the others. When the punk scene began in the mid-1970s, the rockers were long established in the clubs.

The music scene was soon affected by the country's rising unemployment and increased immigration, and in short order, the rockers became divided. Some remained biracial and became known as the "2 tones," antiracist skinheads who favored Jamaican reggae music. The other skinheads became anti-Semitic and anti-immigration, expressing their philosophy through frequent attacks on immigrants. Even though the two groups had gone in opposite directions philosophically, they both developed a liking for Oi music.

The racist skinheads found a special appeal with Oi music. In particular they liked the simple melodies, the chanting lyrics, and violent, thumping beat. They considered the sound clean, pure, and simple, like their racist philosophy.

When skinheads began appearing in the United States in the early 1980s, music—Oi music in particular—was already part of their scene. The largest problem skinheads had was finding recordings. Bootlegged copies of Skrewdriver's records sold in Los Angeles for $100. When they couldn't find white power music, they went to clubs where heavy-metal groups were playing for minorities and antiracist skins. Clashes would break out between the two groups, a phenomenon that continues to this day.

Today

The early music is still popular today. Songs such as "White Rider," "White Warrior," "The New Storm Troopers," "Take the Sword," "Fists of Steel," "Heads Kicked In," "Reich 'n' Roll," and "Blood and Honor" pretty much sum up the content of the music.

The names of the groups also leave little doubt as to what they are about. From the United Kingdom there are The Klansmen, Brutal Attack, Sudden Impact, Elite Terror, Skrewdriver, No Remorse, and Public Enemy. From France there are the Evil Skins, Brutal Combat, Warrior Kids, and Legion SS. In the United States we have The Kicker Boys, Doc Martens, Anti Heroes, and Bound for Glory.

Skrewdriver is probably held in highest esteem both in England and the United States, despite the fact the the group is unable to come to America because of its members' criminal records—which is probably a good thing considering the impact they would have here. As mentioned, it's hard to find their albums and tapes in this country, and those skinheads who possess them prize them as highly as gold. The following is a sampling of lyrics from some of Skrewdriver's greatest hits:

Strikeforce, white survival, strikeforce
Strikeforce kill all rivals
(from "Strike Force")

We will fight against them with a hammer and a gun
And when our people start to rise, the traitors'
time will come.
(from "Power from Profit")

We live on the streets now; we fight for our lives,
We fight for the flag, we are all willing to die.
(from "Flying the Flag")

The music of Ken Death, who is now serving a life sentence for murder, was never known for its subtlety:

Victims all around me
I feel nothing but hate
Bashing their brains in
is my only trade.

Senseless violence is the only thing I know.
Piles of corpses never ending, watch them grow.
Kill my victims for pleasure and for fun
Beat them over the head, shoot them with my gun.

Line them up against a wall.
Shoot them watch them die.
I love to hear the agony.
They vomit, scream, and cry.

Senseless violence is my favorite game.
If everyone dies I am not to blame.
Burn their smelling corpses into the ground.
I will make sure nobody is to be found.

You Just Gotta Go Listen

It's a good idea for local police to monitor all concerts featuring slam dancing music. An informant's tip about a possible fight between opposing skinhead gangs usually has some validity and warrants police attention. Fights may take place inside the concert hall, while other times they will occur out on the sidewalk or in the parking lot. Watch for weapons, especially when the skins are outside where they have quick and easy access to their vehicles. Wanted skinheads frequently go to concerts. It's a good idea to have several officers on the scene when an arrest goes down since the skinheads' peers will most likely interfere. Tip: If you have to spend much time inside the concert hall, wear ear plugs.

GRAFFITI

Bloods, Crips, and Hispanic gangs have interesting, stylistic, sometimes even pretty graffiti, which may take all of your imagination to decipher, if you can at all. You may be able to figure out the author's alphabet, but the message may still be so cryptic that its meaning is impossible to guess.

This is not the case with skinhead graffiti. They leave their mark with simplistic, basic, and straight-to-the-point mesages. You don't have to do a lot of head scratching to guess what is meant by such scrawlings as the following:

- Fuck Niggers
- Gooks Out
- Jews Die
- Kill Fags
- Nazis Rule
- White Power

Like other gangs, skinheads use graffiti to mark their territory. If a specific skinhead gang (e.g., Hitler's Boys) lives primarily on the east side of town, you're going to see its name marked mostly on the east side of town. Gangs that are large, that have members who live all over the city, will write their name over a much larger area.

Marking their territory, however, is not the motivating factor behind most skinhead graffiti. Most often they spray a wall because it's the best place to do it at that particular moment. Remember, they're not into a lot of planning.

From time to time, they will deface specific targets, such as a black-owned business or a Jewish synagogue. On the black-owned business they will write something like "Niggers Out"; on the synagogue they will scrawl "Hitler Lives." Most of the time, the writing will be on one of the exterior walls, but if they break in, they may mark it on an inside one as well.

Which brings up another issue. Sometimes burglars will scrawl white supremacy slogans and symbols inside homes or businesses to throw suspicion on a skinhead. Most of the time, the informed investigator can detect that

Typical skin-head graffiti emphasize white power, nazism, and their equipment.

the markings and writings are not those of a person who is a true believer. The most obvious sign that the burglar is not a white supremacist is an incorrectly drawn swastika, usually drawn backward, as if you were looking at it in a mirror. If there is one thing a neo-Nazi skinhead knows how to do, it's how to draw a swastika correctly.

> A black woman reported to the police that someone had written the words "Nigger" and the letters "W.A.R." on the side of her house—obviously an acronym for Tom Metzger's White Aryan Resistance organization. However, white supremacists write the acronym without the periods: WAR. The investigation subsequently revealed the woman had mental problems and had written on the wall to draw attention.

(This will be discussed further in Chapter 5, "Hate Crime Hoaxes.")

Cars frequently provide skinheads with another canvas on which they can express their views. A mixed-race couple may find a swastika, "KKK," or "Nigger Lover" etched in their car's paint.

Although white supremacy graffiti often contain satanic verses or symbols, you shouldn't automatically jump to the conclusion that you are dealing with satanists. Some skinheads are heavily into satanism, some just dabble, and some may simply like satanic art and use it in their graffiti.

Legally, graffiti are considered a hate crime when the motive is to intimidate the victim because of his or her race, ethnicity, sexual orientation, religious views, etc. Writing on someone's wall may not seem like a heavy-duty crime, but it can be psychologically traumatic to the victim and the community.

POSTERS, FLIERS, AND STICKERS

Although the media are the best source of advertising for skinheads and other white supremacists, the gangs still use various types of literature to intimidate, inform, and spread propaganda. They staple posters on walls and telephone poles and glue them on windows. Fliers are placed behind windshield wipers, on doorsteps, and in mail slots and are handed out on street corners and at public events. Stickers are most often found stuck on glass, such as car windshields and store windows.

Stickers can be purchased through such white supremacy newspapers as Tom Metzger's *WAR*. Five dollars will buy a roll of 100 or more, an inexpensive price when you consider that many people will see one sticker and potentially be affected by it. Now that we are in the computer age and desktop publishing is common, some skinhead groups are creating their own stickers, complete with their group's name and mailing address on the bottom. Although they are in black and white and lack the gloss of the professional stickers, the message, the all-important message, is still the same.

Fliers and posters can also be bought through white supremacist newspapers, but again desktop publishing has opened a whole world of creativity and convenience for skinheads, allowing them to instantaneously come up with a greater variety than ever before. Some fliers and posters have been around for many years, showing up in their original form or modified to fit the needs of the distributors. With a pair of scissors and a coping machine, skins can create an infinite variety of forms, all of which have the distributor's post office box on the bottom.

The All-Important Message

Fliers and posters often encourage whites to wake up to what is happening to their country. They criticize minorities, Jews, and homosexuals. They depict cartoon caricatures of minorities with exaggerated features and drawings of well-muscled skinheads posing like young, strong soldiers, reminiscent of paintings from World War II Germany and Mao's Red China.

One skinhead gang distributed the following flier, complete with two group photos of members and their

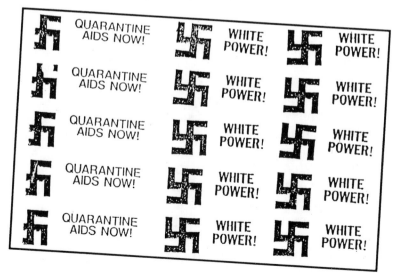

Pages of stickers such as these can be purchased by the hundreds for only a few dollars.

post office box at the bottom. (The punctuation and capitalization are theirs.)

> SKINHEADS OF AMERICA, like the dynamic skinheads in Europe, are working class Aryan Youth. We oppose the capitalist and the communist scum that are destroying our Aryan race. We also realize that the parasitic Jewish race is at the heart of our problem, along with the race traitors of our own race, who willingly do the Jew bidding.
>
> SKINHEADS worldwide are warriors. We never run away, back down, or sell out. We despise the traitors, the cowards, the apathetic, and the limp wristed queers. We will fight forever to defend our people and our land. Our heads are shaved for battle.
>
> SKINHEADS believe in the virtues of hard work. We believe that motherhood is the greatest and most noble position to which any white woman can aspire. We also believe in the family, with a dominate male and proud female, as the best way to insure proper reproduction of our race.
>
> SKINHEADS are activists. We are at war with the system and the commies. This battle will receive our full attention.

As will all propaganda, skinhead posters and fliers serve different purposes. Sometimes they comment on current news stories that reinforce skin philosophy. Oftentimes a newspaper clipping will be copied onto the page.

Some fliers are distributed solely for their shock value. Fliers, such as one depicting a large photo of Adolph Hitler's face, with bold caps declaring, "Next Time: No More Mr. Nice Guy," or one that shows a picture of a microwave oven with the banner "For Short Jews" serve no other function than to shock and intimidate.

Other fliers are used to educate, such as one that had a newspaper article about a drive-by shooting by a black gang. The flier's bold caption read: "Black Gangs Are Ruining Our Cities."

Such fliers and posters are effective when seen by cer-

Typical skinhead fliers distributed by racist skinheads to spread their message.

Why White Nationalism?

According to **Time** magazine, April 9, 1990, in the cover story "Beyond the Melting Pot": "Already one American in four defines himself or herself as Hispanic or non-white. If current trends in immigration and birth rates persist, the Hispanic population will have further increased an estimated 21%, the Asian presence about 22%, Blacks almost 12% and Whites a little more than 2% when the 20th Century ends. By 2020 the number of U.S. residents who are Hispanic or non-white will have more than doubled, to nearly 115 million, while the white population will not be increasing at all.... By 2056 whites may be a minority group."

Yes, Whites will become a minority group and how will they be treated by the non-White majority? Will the non-White majority allow them to form a powerful minority political organization? Will they give poor Whites welfare, food stamps and allow them to suck it up on the dole? Or will they cast our descendants into a kind of slavery - to pay for the "sins of the past," of course. Or perhaps, after years of being taught that Whites were the "haters and persecutors of mankind," they will simply slaughter our descendants as they have done to the Whites in Africa.

Multiracialism and increased non-White immigration are the policies not just of the United States. Multiracialism is now promoted by almost every White government in the world: Canada, Australia, Britain, Italy, Germany, the Soviet Union, etc., etc. And any White who disagrees with this spectacle of human lemmings rushing to the sea is condemned and persecuted as a "racist." Yet, all other races have nations to protect their racial and cultural integrity. Israel is for the Jews, Japan for the Japanese, Kenya for the Blacks and so on. Only the

Whites can have no country that will protect their identity and ensure their survival as a people - for that would be "racist." In their grand hypocrisy the Capitalists and the Communists and the Jews have one set of standards for White people and another set for the other races. As the White world slips further into the dark abyss of multiracialism and multiculturalism will not our culture and our Race cease to exist? We have already become a people without a country - we have been stripped of our racial and cultural identity and soon we will be subsumed within the multiracial mass! Is this what you want for your children and their children? No? **Then it is time to fight!**

tain people, especially impressionable young people, who need to blame someone for some perceived injustice in their lives. For example, a white street kid who gets his backpack stolen one night by a couple of black street thugs, then the next day gets handed a skinhead flier that reads "Niggers Are Thieves," is likely to agree and seek out more information.

Some posters, fliers, and stickers do not list a post office box or recorded message number. They are distributed only for propaganda purposes. Most of them, however, do have follow-up addresses and phone numbers where people can seek out additional information. These are for recruiting purposes or so people can send money to the listed post office box. There are people out there, blue-collar workers and white-collar professionals, who secretly applaud what white supremacists advocate and quietly support the movement with money.

> One neo-Nazi skinhead reported that her organization receives $5, $10, and $20 contributions in their post office box regularly. She said it's almost always in cash, so the contributors remain anonymous.

It's important for the investigating officer to remember that even though in most cases the distribution of the literature is not a crime, it can nonetheless be devastating to a targeted person or group. When a Jewish person receives a flier proclaiming the Holocaust did not occur, or that it should happen again, the investigating officer needs to be sensitive to the person's emotional state.

ANTIRACIST SKINHEADS

It has been Portland's experience that the antiracist skinheads are just as violent as the racist—at times, even more so. Their primary target is anyone they perceive as racist, in particular, a neo-Nazi skinhead.

Antiracist gangs use a variety of names—Racial Unity

Skin Heads, Anti-Racist Action, Two-Tone Skins, and Mad-Skins, but SHARP (Skinheads against Racial Prejudice) is probably the most recognized moniker and, as far as law enforcement is concerned, has become almost a generic term for antiracist skinheads.

In the Beginning

In 1987 there was a weak, short-lived group in Portland calling itself SCAR (Skinheads Committed against Racism), which did little more than staple its posters to telephone poles. But in early 1990, at a time when the racist skins were getting a lot of media attention, SHARP antiracist skinheads appeared on the scene, formed mostly from local street people and a few out-of-towners. They looked the same as the racist skins except for patches and tattoos that proclaimed their antiracist philosophy.

They immediately got the attention of the media, going as far as calling their own press conferences and getting reporters to go on "patrol" with them as they walked along the mean streets looking for Nazis. They told the press they were going to rid Portland of racist gangs, although the means they were going to use to accomplish this task were never clearly stated.

To the uneducated eye, this seemed a good idea. The same people who worked diligently to try and stop Bloods and Crips from killing each other thought it was a blessing that the SHARPs were taking it upon themselves to use whatever means necessary to stop white, racist skinheads. One professional, highly educated black activist said publicly that SHARPs were a good idea because he had heard that in another city SHARPs had driven the racist skins out through violent means. (I wanted to ask if that meant we could use the Bloods in the same way to drive the Crips out of town, but I didn't.)

The police were not fooled by the SHARPs' posturing. We knew that most of the SHARPs were downtown street kids with rap sheets from here to there. It was obvious

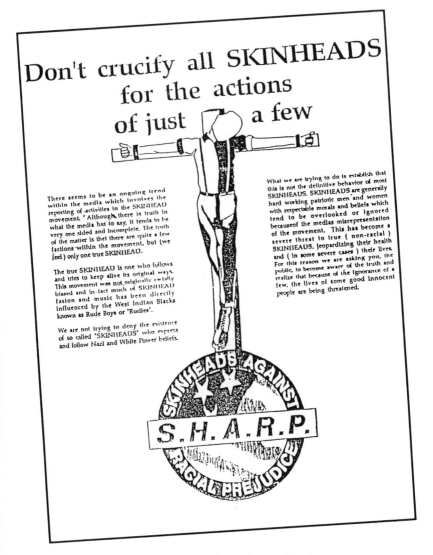

Don't crucify all SKINHEADS
for the actions
of just   a few

There seems to be an ongoing trend within the media which involves the reporting of activities in the SKINHEAD movement. Although there is truth in what the media has to say, it tends to be very one sided and incomplete. The truth of the matter is that there are quite a few factions within the movement, but (we feel) only one true SKINHEAD.

The true SKINHEAD is one who follows and tries to keep alive its original ways. This movement was not originally racially biased and in fact much of SKINHEAD fasion and music has been directly influenced by the West Indian Blacks known as Rude Boys or "Rudies".

We are not trying to deny the existence of so called "SKINHEADS" who express and follow Nazi and White Power beliefs.

What we are trying to do is establish that this is not the definitive behavior of most SKINHEADS. SKINHEADS are generally hard working patriotic men and women with respectable morals and beliefs which tend to be overlooked or ignored because of the medias misrepresentation of the movement. This has become a severe threat to true (non-racial) SKINHEADS, jeopardizing their health and (in some severe cases) their lives. For this reason we are asking you, the public, to become aware of the truth and realize that because of the ignorance of a few, the lives of some good innocent people are being threatened.

SKINHEADS AGAINST

S.H.A.R.P.

RACIAL PREJUDICE

An antiracist flier distributed by SHARPs to inform the public about the difference between the two factions of skinheads.

ONE RACE, THE HUMAN RACE

We all see the trend in shaved heads lately. A shaved means that you are racist, fascist, and stupid. A shaved head means your trying to look tough. A shaved head means you are gonna fight in groups. A shaved head means no fun at shows. But, I want to point out that a shaved head doesn't mean a skinhead. Any nazi scum could shave their head, but would that make them a skinhead? No, it wouldn't! A skinhead is a young, working class man or woman who identifys with the lifestyle of the original skinhead movement. That is, be proud of what you are and stick together through it all no matter what may be your way. Stand your ground and have fun doing it.

But now we have kids shaving their heads, buying boots and bombers, and acting real mean like killing people and calling themselves skinheads. Not are they only dressing in the skinhead "style", but these hicks are also allowing themselves to be used by white power and neo-nazi organizations as easly recruited followers. Whose fault is this? Is it the media's fault for showing very few skins that are not racist, not showing both sides of the coin? Is it the racist organizer's fault for bribing the young skin with leadership and a sense of bogus values so they will perform the organizers dirty work? Or is it the fault of the nonracist skins who refuse to accept the new skins and force them to seek acceptance with bald nazi scum? The answer is that it is a combination of all these factors. A racist does not make a good skin simply because ignorance doesn't make a good skin. It is the responsibility of all to make racism mixed with the skinhead movement unpopular and unacceptable. A shaved head is now seen by the public as the same thing as a klansman's hood or a swastika armband. I don't want that and I know many others that feel the same way.

IT'S UP TO US.

S.C.A.R.
Skinheads Committed Against Racism

A.R.A.
Anti Racist Action

A antiracist flier distributed in Portland that attempted to explain the difference between skinheads.

they loved the attention, and it was apparent they were going to act out to keep the attention coming.

Joining Forces with the Left Wing

Initially, SHARPs aligned themselves with left-wing activist groups, such as gay rights organizations, assorted antiracist activists, and many others. These groups were also fooled by the SHARPs, welcoming them into their ranks and even employing them as security for their demonstrations and marches.

Within just a few weeks, however, SHARPs began showing their true colors. They committed assault, intimidation, harassment, and drive-by shootings. We reported this to the press, but certain activist groups still refused to believe it. One very large organization, a coalition representing social worker groups and activists from all over the West, went so far as to say that the police were lying about the SHARPs' criminal activities.

Eventually some of these groups began to see for themselves that SHARP was a violent street gang. Suddenly the antiracist skinheads found that they were no longer included in the activities of the activist organizations. At the same time, the police had gathered enough information to arrest many SHARPs, including the leader, who had smashed a young girl in the head with a hammer because he thought she was a Nazi. With his 14-month jail sentence, SHARP, as an organization, collapsed.

It's important to keep in mind that when a gang structure dissolves, there are still ex-members around. They might act independently for a while, or they might start working immediately to get another gang together. In either case, you need to keep tabs on them.

> "I don't think they actually know what they are fighting for," one racist skinhead leader said. "They don't have that fire burning inside of them. Their purpose is to hate us. They don't even take a antiracist stand. They just want to fight racist skinheads."

Antiracist skinheads, along with anarchists, throwing stones at the police.

•

As this text was in production, two rival Portland skinhead gangs met in a snow-covered parking lot to fight. Unknown to the racist skinheads, one of the antiracist skins brought an SKS assault rifle. After several shots were fired, one racist skin lay dead with a round through his forehead.

•

"Friends of mine are stocking up on guns and some other kinds of weapons," said an antiracist skin. "If Nazis are going to try to start a race war or intimidate their opponents, they're going to have a hell of a fight."

The police are often just as much a target of antiracists' venom as the racist skins. One antiracist publication's banner began: "Stop Killer Cops! Smash the Klan!"

"We can't depend on the cops or the government to fight racism," antiracists have said. "We must educate and mobilize inside our communities because the cops and Klan work hand in hand."

•

As police officers in a major city attempted to arrest two SHARP skinheads, they were struck with rocks, bottles, and pieces of pipe.

Racist skinheads proclaim the death of SHARP and punctuate it with a swastika.

Many serious racist skinheads are willing to die in support of white power.

Antiracist skinheads are not going away. It's important for law enforcement to monitor their activity and know that they are just as much a threat as the racist skins.

ALLEGIANCE

As mentioned elsewhere, some hard-core skinheads will die in support of their racist beliefs. The white supremacy philosophy is so entrenched in their minds, indeed their genes, that they are willing to defend it to the death.

Others—though they may wear flight jackets, Doc Martens, and white power tattoos on the sides of their necks—do not possess such deep-seated beliefs. They may appear hard-core, but they can be influenced to get out of the racist movement or switch their allegiance to antiracist skins.

> Mark is 22 years old and has been a skinhead for five years. He's been both a White Power skin and a SHARP.
>
> Mark started out as a racist skin, but when the SHARPs began to get a lot of media attention, he switched over. He stayed in that capacity for two years, but when they began to dissolve and a particularly active racist skinhead was getting notice, Mark switched back. A few months later when his mentor was sentenced to two years for assault, he donned his SHARP patch again. When last contacted, he was still wearing the SHARP patch, but just in case, he had a shoulder patch of a racist organization in his pocket.

The Iffy Ones

Some skinheads will give up their life-style, racist or nonracist, if something better comes along. These types just experiment until they find their right niche, which could be religion, a well-paying job, a lover, or just the realization that being a skinhead is a dead-end place to be.

Most of them, however, stay involved. They may become inactive, at least as far as contact with the police is concerned, but then after awhile their names begin to show up in police reports again. This could be the result of making contact with other skins or an event that sparked a renewed interest in the white supremacy movement.

> Adam had been with a skinhead gang for three years. He ran with 25 others, committing the usual crimes of graffiti, intimidation, and assault. Then he dropped out of sight. There were rumors he had gone to England or moved to a new state. Then after a year of not hearing anything about Adam, he was arrested in Sandpoint, Idaho, for the shooting death of another skinhead. Two months earlier, Adam had moved to the Aryan Nations' compound in Hayden Lake. A few weeks later, he and another skinhead had killed a fellow skin and buried the body in the snow.

Oftentimes, when they reappear on the scene, they are more active than they were the first time. In fact, it's not uncommon for them to come back in a leadership capacity, that is, as much leadership as there is among authority-hating skinheads.

The Hard-Core Racists

The true hard-core racist skins are those who have been around for a long time and have never changed their beliefs, and they more than likely never will. They are entrenched. Perhaps they were raised that way, or perhaps their life experiences led them to their racist philosophy. How they got to where they are is more of an issue for the social workers to look at. The fact that they are hard-core and act out on it criminally is the concern of law enforcement.

SKINHEAD INTELLECT

One of the things people notice immediately when they meet and talk with skinheads for the first time is that they are not very bright. I don't know how many times reporters have called me after having interviewed skin-heads and said, "They're really stupid, aren't they?"

It may seem that most of them are as dumb as a house plant, but there are also those who are quite knowledge-able, although it's usually limited to white supremacy issues. The brightest are usually in some sort of leader-ship capacity.

One 22-year-old female, Anne, is particularly brilliant in the area of local, national, and international politics. She has a large library of books on racism, World War II, Hitler, and the Nazi movement. She even has a working knowledge of the German language. During the years I have known her, she has always been the leader, the organizer, never a follower.

Her love life, however, has been a series of bad, if not dumb, choices. When I first met her she was engaged to be married to a young man who was serving a couple of years in an east coast prison. They planned to build a house in the woods and raise six little Aryan babies, with German names she had already picked out. A few months later it was over, and she was suddenly engaged to a man serving a sentence in a Wyoming prison, a man she had only met through letters. They too had big plans, but plans that had to wait for six years until he got out. That lasted just a short while, then she landed a young man who was still in high school. They wanted to live together and fight together for the white race, but his parents wouldn't let him leave.

•

As the police handcuffed a heavily tattooed skinhead, the skin repeatedly shouted, "I'm a Nazi! I'm a Nazi!" Later, when the officers asked him what he thought a Nazi was, he admitted he had no idea.

•

A skinhead who beat a man to death had just two years earlier been an outstanding student and the president of his high school. When the judge sentenced him to 20 years, the 20-year-old skin read a statement so brilliantly written that it could have come from an eloquent attorney.

Many skinheads have trouble stringing together two coherent sentences. The depth of their understanding of the very thing they are supposed to represent goes no deeper than a slogan printed on one of the fliers they place on windshields. They say are Nazis, but they are unable to converse on the history of Nazism.

There are others in the movement who truly believe in what they are doing and work hard to educate themselves through reading and learning by any means they can. They believe in the power of knowledge. It's not too unreasonable to assume that, as the movement continues and as more educated people become involved in it, they will begin to use criminal and civil laws to their advantage.

For every smart and informed skinhead, there are 10 who could care less about learning what it is they represent. They are simply involved in it for the violence and the gang atmosphere. While some of the less intelligent are easily controlled within the gang, some are not. Both kinds are dangerous.

TYPES OF SKINHEAD GANG MEMBERS

Wannabe

A wannabe is generally defined as a person who dresses and acts like a skinhead because he wants to be one. Some parents, social workers, and other people with their heads in the sand use this term as a way of saying, "Oh, he's just a mischievous young man. He's just acting out and sowing his wild oats." Baloney. This term does not make any sense. If the kid looks like one and acts act like one, then he is one.

Fence Straddler

As already discussed, some skinheads can't decide whether they want to be racist or antiracist. During the summer, they run with the racists, and during the winter, they switch allegiance to the antiracists. Some skinheads switch because one side is getting more attention than

Skinheads are often accused of not being very intelligent.

the other. Some even own patches, pins, and papers representing both sides, so they can switch whenever they need to.

Associate

An associate is a person involved with a gang to a lesser degree than the hard-core skin. He will be active for a few months, drop out, then reappear on the scene. Oftentimes, his appearance will be ambiguous, displaying some but not all skinhead affectations, such as having a full head of hair, Nike shoes, but wearing a flight jacket. He might have "SKINHEAD" tattooed on one arm, but wear a dress shirt and a pair of slacks. An associate might wear all his skinhead regalia on Friday and Saturday nights, but then dress normally during the week so he can work as a waiter at the Hilton.

The associate will interact with the hard-core skins and go along with all the things they do. The primary difference is that the associate's involvement is only part-time, both physically and emotionally. He moves in and out of the movement as his needs or the situation dictates.

While there are some females who are definitely hard-core, many females are associated with skinhead gangs simply because they like a guy who is a member. There are skin girls who will tell you they "sorta" believe in the philosophy, although it appears they are just going along with the gang for the excitement and because that is where the boys are.

Hard-Core

The definition of a hard-core gang member is a person completely immersed in the skinhead gang/white supremacy life-style and philosophy. He has never been a fence straddler and has never deviated from his beliefs and goals. Unless there are extenuating circumstances, the hard-core skinhead will always have a shaved head or, at the very least, short hair. He will almost always wear a flight jacket, Doc Marten boots, and lots of patches and tattoos. He will profess his philosophy at the least provocation and will frequently distribute fliers and leaflets in plain view of the public. When approached by the police, he will freely admit what he is and what he believes.

> A 20-year-old hard-core skinhead and member of the KKK stood tall as the judge sentenced him to 10 years in prison. When the judge completed his remarks, the skinhead stood in defiant attention, his chin raised high. Then without saying a word, he raised his arm in the Nazi salute.
>
> •
>
> A skinhead girl was in the courtroom listening to the judge read the conditions of her probation. When the hearing was over, she walked to the door, turned back to the bench, and snapped out a Nazi salute, shouting, "Sieg Heil!"

Most hard-core skinheads have been involved in the white supremacy movement for a long time, and their life-style reflects it. For example, a skinhead's apartment will be a tribute to his beliefs. The walls will be covered with posters and snapshots depicting Adolph Hitler, Skrewdriver, and various skinhead activities. Nazi flags will adorn one wall and a Confederate flag another. There will be books and tapes on white supremacy and Christian Identity lying around.

The hard-core skinhead is so entrenched in his beliefs that it's hard to imagine him not being a racist and belonging to some organization his entire life. He will probably die shouting, "White power!"

SKINHEADS AND OTHER GANGS

Since the beginning of the gang problem, officers have been asked a thousand times, "Why don't you cops just put all these gang punks out on an island and let them kill each other?"

One man had a slight twist to the idea: "Put all the Bloods, Crips, Southeast Asians, Hispanics, skinheads, and whatever other gangsters there are into a huge stadium, and let them have at it. Park a cop car outside to listen, like he was listening to a bag of microwave popcorn popping away. Then when the officer hears the last pop, he can go in and arrest the last gangster."

Although it would seem that the various gangs would be natural enemies, it's rare for skinheads to clash with any of them. Most of the Bloods, Crips, Hispanics, and Southeast Asians are too busy wheeling and dealing guns and narcotics to bother seeking out skinheads to fight.

When it does occur, however, it can be violent.

> Three skinheads were standing outside of a teen night club when a Toyota containing six Southeast Asian gangsters, dressed in their colors, passed slowly along the curb. The skinheads shouted out, "Gook!" and taunted them to stop and fight. The Toyota continued at the same slow pace along the curb, turned the corner, and disappeared. As the skinheads lit fresh cigarettes and laughed about scaring off the "gooks," the Toyota rounded the corner behind them and crept slowly along the curb again. As the skinheads turned to see the car, an Asian gangster leaned out the passenger window and fired a semiautomatic weapon, striking the closest skinhead in the groin.

> •

> The mother and her sleepy 10-year-old daughter were enjoying the otherwise empty car to themselves as the light rail train moved through the late night streets. The quiet was suddenly interrupted as 10 to 15 blacks burst through the doors, shouting and cursing. All were wearing red, colors of the Blood gang. A moment later, 20 skinheads rushed through the doors, obviously in pursuit of the Bloods. The mother and daughter clung desperately to each other as the rival gangs punched, kicked, and grappled. The fight was so fierce that witnesses on the sidewalk said the car rocked on its tracks. At one point during the battle, the young girl cried out to her mother, "Mommy, are we going to die?"

> •

> Two black youths, admitted members of the Crips, were walking along a railroad track outside

an amusement park at midnight. As they passed a mud puddle, a rock landed in the water and splashed them. Looking toward the top of an embankment they saw three figures in the dark. When the Crips taunted them to fight, the three figures rushed down the bank. As they got closer, the Crips realized the three were skinheads. It also became suddenly apparent there were others, as about 40 skinheads stepped out from behind shrubs and trees. The Crips were beaten and stabbed, one nearly dying from loss of blood.

•

"Ah, I see your life-style finally caught up with you," one policeman said to a skinhead who had been shot in the stomach by a black gang member.

Skinheads speak critically of the other gangs, but for the most part they're grudgingly respectful of them. One skinhead said, "We don't want to fight them because they've got automatic weapons." Another skinhead said they like the violence that happens between the other gangs because they are only killing themselves, which means there will be fewer muds.

At several high schools, fliers appeared thanking Bloods and Crips for killing each other and reducing the black population. This reduction of blacks, the flier said, would result in less competition in the job market. At the bottom of the document was a post office box of a skinhead/white supremacist organization.

Much of the gang violence among the Bloods, Crips, Southeast Asians, and Hispanics is a result of caustic words, some exchange of disrespectful language, "dis" or "dis'n" as the gangsters call it. To dis one another, the gangs must first have had interaction with one another. As a rule, skinheads do not hang out in the same places as the other gangs, so these confrontations seldom occur. On those rare occasions when they do clash, as in the scenarios above, you can be guaranteed there will be explosive violence.

CHAPTER 3

I t may be true that skinheads are off in their own little world, but it is not necessary that law enforcement officers tiptoe around them. Keep in mind, most skinheads are just kids, albeit with a peculiar philosophy and a propensity for violence. With some exceptions, they like to talk about what they do. When a kid hits a home run, he likes to tell everyone about it. When he stomps around in big boots and a shaved head terrorizing people, he likes to talk about that too.

Occasionally, however, a skinhead will stand in front of you with shaved head, boots, swastika tattoos on his face, and a flight jacket and deny he has anything to do with being a racist skin. He will say he just dresses that way because he likes the style, or he wears the boots because they are comfortable, or he found the jacket in a trash can. He is lying of course, but he will not change his story no matter how much you point out the inconsistencies in it.

GETTING THEM TO TALK

Sometimes you might have to break the ice to get him to talk.

The skinhead sat in the jail holding room, his arms folded across his chest and his lips forming a tight, determined line. His head was clean

WHAT COPS SHOULD KNOW ABOUT SKINHEADS

shaven, and he wore a white T-shirt, jeans, and Doc Martens. His T-shirt depicted a hand-painted pistol firing a round through a man's forehead, with blood and brain matter blowing out the back of the man's head across the T-shirt's front and shoulder.

The officer tried in vain to get him to talk, to respond in any fashion to his questions, but the skin sat stone-faced, staring straight ahead. Attempting a little flattery, the officer complimented the T-shirt's artistic merits, its rich, red color and the realistic expression of shock on the man's face.

At first the skinhead's eyelids fluttered, as if he was coming out of a trance, then his face brightened and a big smile spread from ear to ear. He began to point out some of the painting's finer points, then went on to talk about his girlfriend, who had painted it. For the next hour, the skinhead was a virtual talking machine, only stopping occasionally to take a breath.

De-Cop Yourself

The old adage "you can catch more flies with honey than vinegar" applies to skinheads. They hate authority. To get information, you have to "de-cop" yourself. If you try to talk with a skinhead while wearing your mirrored sunglasses and a Smokey hat, bracing your shiny boot on the police car bumper, and holding a notebook in your hand, the skinhead is either going to clam up or lie through his teeth.

When your contact is merely conversational, the gentle approach works best (befitting the 1990s philosophy of kinder and gentler police officers). Street clothes are preferable, but if that is impossible, then an easygoing demeanor and, what all police euphemistically term, "bullshit ability" will go a long way toward breaking the ice.

Separate to Weaken

When there is more than one skinhead, separate them. You take one, and your partner gets one. As a general rule, skinheads need the presence of their comrades to show off their bravado and be flippant. When they are by themselves, their courage is "gone with the wind." It's quite common for the toughest-looking skinhead to break into tears when he is alone in an interview room with an officer who is questioning him about his involvement in a crime. Without the skin's peer support base, he crumbles, the warrior dissolves, and the child returns.

When They Want to Talk, Let Them

When asked about their philosophy or politics, skins frequently climb onto a soapbox and begin pontificating. Encourage it. A lot of good information can be gained by listening to what they believe in. As they talk, nod a lot. This is an old trick used by reporters to encourage the interviewee to keep on talking. You should be cautious, however, about agreeing verbally, even though you are doing it just to encourage conversation. The racist skinhead, or any witnesses, might use it against you later by reporting to your superiors, internal affairs, or the press that you share their white supremacy philosophy. Simply nodding your head is easily defensible if accusations are made.

Show Your Knowledge

If you know something about their philosophy and they can see that, they will be encouraged to talk more. When you are able to comment on or ask questions about Aryan Nations, Christian Identity, or the KKK, you are more likely to get good responses. It's simply using good conversational skills: know your subject and you will get more out of the exchange.

Ask them whom they know that you might know. People like to talk about other people. Drop names on them by asking, "Do you like so and so? Do you ever hang out with so and so? Is so and so a racist skin or an antiracist skin? Has so and so committed any crimes?"

Ask Them about Their Enemies

One particularly effective question to ask a skinhead is: "Whom don't you like?" All skinheads have enemies since they fight more among themselves than they do against the hated ZOG. If a skinhead gets an opportunity to burn an enemy, he just might do it. Take advantage of his hate and anger and pump him for what he knows about his enemies. You may just find out who painted the graffiti on the synagogue or who did the cross burning on the black couple's lawn.

Asking them about their enemies is an effective ice breaker, too. A skinhead may be more likely to talk about a gang or a person he dislikes than he is about himself. Once he is talking, you can lead the conversation wherever you want it to go.

Ask about Past and Future Events

Ask about any upcoming events, like a rally, concert, or holiday, such as Martin Luther King, Jr. Day. Most of the time, a skinhead will clam up or be evasive about such events, especially if he is planning on being involved in them. On the other hand, if he isn't going to be involved, or if he knows that a rival skinhead gang will be there, you just might get good intelligence.

Ask about past events. He will probably deny being there, especially if a crime occurred, but if an enemy of his was involved, he might tell you that person's name.

Give Out Your Business Cards

Always give a skinhead your business card. Nine out of 10 will never call you, but that tenth one will when he has something good to tell you.

> When a skinhead was beaten to death by other skinheads, news of the killing spread among the gangs even before the story hit the evening news. Within hours, the investigating officers were bombarded with telephone calls from skinheads informing on other skins. All of the calls came from skinheads who had been given business cards by the officers.

What Do They Think of You?

Ask skinheads what they think of you and what they have heard other skins say about you. When you work around them frequently, especially if you do so aggressively, it's nice to know what kind of reputation you have. Remember, no matter how good a relationship you think you have with them, you are still part of ZOG they so despise.

> One officer spoke congenially with every skinhead he interviewed in jail, and when he spoke with them on the telephone, he always took the time to answer their questions. When he stopped them on the street, he was friendly, and always used an easygoing approach.
>
> One day, while searching through a recently vacated skinhead apartment, the officer found a "hit list" with his name on it, offering a reward of $400 to any skinhead who killed him.

Skinheads frequently keep intelligence information on police officers, especially those who are active. One antiracist gang had files, photos, and computerized information on officers. A racist skinhead gang had a file on an active officer that included his name, age, make and model of his service weapon, and the make and model of his car.

Ask Them about Their Symbolism

Ask about their regalia and accessories, such as jewelry, patches, insignias, tattoos, and anything else attached to their clothing or bodies. When in their apartments, ask the meaning behind things you see on the walls, such as posters, pictures, and flags. Look for items of interest on the floor and on tables, like German and World War II artifacts, books, weapons, and video and audio tapes.

Even if you know what the items are, ask about them anyway. You may learn something new, and at the very least, you will learn what the gang is about. It doesn't hurt to ask them to give you things either, like fliers and newspapers. Sometimes they will give something up, sometimes they will tell you to stuff it.

INFORMANTS

Informants are one of the most important tools you

have for working skinhead gangs. They are a source of all kinds of invaluable information because they are usually in the middle of what is going on. The informant might be associated with a gang, a landlord from an apartment complex where skins live, or the mother of a skinhead who wants her child dissociated from the life-style.

Informants can tell you about upcoming events, such as a rally, concert, or a party at a known skinhead apartment. They can tell you who is going to be there and what is going to happen. Or informants can tell you about past events you might be investigating. They may know who was there and who did what. They probably will not tell you about their friends, but they will talk about their enemies.

They can tell you about new gangs in town and which gangs are rivals. They can provide you with details about a gang's or an individual's philosophy. They can keep you up to date about dress style, new insignias, and where skins are living and hanging out. Informants can let you know what skinheads are saying about you or any other officer.

Keep in mind that when the information sounds extraordinary, it's probably poppycock. Intelligence about hand grenades and .50-caliber machine guns is as common as it is bogus. But then every once in a while it's good.

Why Do Informants Talk?

Informants talk for a variety of reasons. Most often, they call you after a major event, such as an assault or a killing between gangs that is being publicized. Some want revenge on a specific individual. Others like the adventure, sneaking around and snitching to the police. Some do it because the police pay for information.

Generally, it's not important why informants want to provide the police with information. If they want to tell you things, let them talk without asking them why. Asking why just might scare them away.

HANGOUTS

Skinhead hangouts vary from city to city. Generally

skins can be found in parks, concerts, coffee houses, stores that carry their clothing and music, or on street corners.

Racist and antiracist skinheads seldom congregate close to each other. The distance they maintain is directly related to what has been happening between them. If there have been intergang clashes, they will stay away from each other, even to the extent that one gang will control one part of town while the other will hang out in another part. If the situation is extreme, as it is in Portland, one group will claim the city, while the other stays in the suburbs. Although some cities report that their racists hang out on one corner and the antiracists hang out across the street, this close proximity is rare and will quickly change as soon as there is a major clash. If there is an upcoming event that both groups are likely to attend, the police should be present to keep a lid on things.

RESIDENCES

It's easy to pick out which house in the neighborhood belongs to skinheads: the curtains are always drawn, and the yard is always trashed.

They never stay in a house or apartment very long because they inevitably get evicted. They seldom live a quiet, peaceful life, choosing instead a riotous one: late-night drinking and partying, fighting on the sidewalks, running through the streets, whooping, and carrying on. It usually takes only a couple of weekends for them to draw the neighbors' ire and attract the attention of the police. Once the landlord gets involved, either through his own discovery or the police or a neighborhood group giving him a call, an eviction notice soon follows.

This quick turnover of living quarters is one of the reasons it's difficult to keep tab on where skinheads are staying. It would certainly make policing them easier if they would stay in one place for a while, but landlords worry so about the destruction of their property.

Inside their residences, skins adorn the walls with flags, posters, and pictures, along with such graffiti as "Death to Race Mixers!" "White Power Rules," "Bound for Glory," and "People Suck." Reggae or white power music is usually blaring loudly. Beer bottles are scattered throughout the living quarters, cigarette smoke is thick as a London fog, and there are enough junk-food wrappers lying about to pack a landfill. If they know the police are coming over, they will hide or remove their weapons, or they will lay their legal weapons out in plain sight to show their openness with the police.

Even though there will be only one or two people on the rental agreement, there will usually be six or seven others illegally living on the premises. That is important to keep in mind for two reasons. First, having extra people living in the rental is a violation and a tool you can use to get the landlord to make an eviction. Second, you always want to take backup along with you when you go to the house or apartment to serve a warrant or just interview someone.

That brings up one final point: skinheads are night owls. If you are going to arrest one at his residence, go at 9:00 A.M. and catch him in bed.

WHEN SKINHEADS GET ARRESTED

When a skinhead gets arrested, he is like any other criminal when it comes to snitching on his comrades. If you put enough pressure on him, he is going to point a quick finger at all the others who were with him during the commission of his crime.

> Four members of the Northeast Boots were arrested for five felonies each after they robbed two white men of their beer; then punched, kicked, and beat the men with the bottles and sliced one victim from ear to mouth with a knife. During the interview, two of the suspects immediately implicated the third as the one who had used the knife. The accused refused to talk to the police, even though he knew his buddies were being charged with the stabbing.

It's a good idea to recontact the arrested skinhead a

week or two after his incarceration to see if he would like to add anything to his statement. He may not involve his comrades right away, but once he has experienced the unpleasantness of jail life, and he realizes that his comrades—his fellow warriors he was convinced would stick with him through thick and thin—are not helping him out, he will often sing like a canary.

Sometimes a skin will switch allegiance to save his butt.

> Brett was a skinny, 17-year-old skinhead, with bulging eyes and a bobbing Adam's apple. He ran with racist skins and told everyone in his grandiose style that when the race war began, he would be right in there "kicking ass and killin' niggers." After he was arrested one night for curfew, he was placed into a holding room with several black gang members. When the heavy door clanged shut, Brett slowly looked around the room, his eyes bulging even more and his Adam's apple pumping like a piston in a race car. Realizing the guacamole was about to hit the fan, he just barely squeaked out, "Yo, dudes! What's up? I'm a SHARP. I'm with you."

WEAPONS

Generally, skinheads do not have the weapons that Southeast Asian and black gangs have. Whereas other gangs prefer semiauto handguns, MAC-10s, and Uzis, skinheads are content with baseball bats or heavy chains.

Baseball Bats

Although there has never been a statistical analysis on skinhead weapons, a safe guess is that a high percentage of their assaults have been committed with baseball bats.

> When a police officer asked a skinhead motorist why there was a baseball bat in the front seat of his car, the skin replied, "You never know when someone will want to play ball in the park." When the officer asked him where his ball and glove were, the skinhead just shrugged and smiled.

*Weapons favored by skinheads. Skinheads usually do not have the
firearms other gangs do.*

A wooden or aluminum baseball bat, swung even by
the scrawniest skinhead, can still cause serious pain and
injury. A bat is cheap compared to a 9mm, and it doesn't
require training for the operator to be effective with it; a
blow from a bat hurts wherever it makes contact.

Possession of a bat is not against the law. Unlike a
firearm, it's even legal to carry in a vehicle—some skins
display one or more prominently in their pickup gun
rack. A skin can even carry one as he walks around
through the streets. A police officer may take it away from
him, especially if he is carrying it at three in the morning,
but unless the skin was threatening or assaulting someone
with it, he can't be charged with its possession.

A wooden bat will sometimes have pertinent intelligence information written on it or carved into it.
Commonly, the gang's name will be found on it, as well as
a roll call of names, such as White Dave, Jason the Basher,
or Puke. This can be incriminating in court, especially if
White Dave just assaulted someone with it. Other markings, such as swastikas and words like "White Power,"

"Nigger Thumper," or "Fag Killer" will typically be found on their bats. Such writing makes a big impact on juries.

Other Clubbing Devices

Other clubbing devices are popular, too, like police batons, table legs, 2x4s, pipes, chains, and maces (not the spray mace but the club with protruding spikes). These are commonly found in their vehicles, apartments, and under their flight jackets. As with bats, these devices are marked with their owners' names and expressions of their philosophy.

Their Doc Marten boots should also be included in a discussion of clubbing devices. The boots are heavy, hard, and most have steel toes. Skinheads love to kick with them, especially after their victim has been knocked to the ground. There have been cases where skins have beaten someone to the sidewalk, performed a "boot party," and left, only to return in a short while to kick the victim again.

> Two skinheads knocked a man down in the street on a stormy December night and executed a boot party on him. Fortunately for the victim, police officers rounded the corner on routine patrol, arrested the two skins, and transported them to the police station. It was a busy Saturday night, which meant the jail was full. The officers wrote the suspects citations to appear in court and confiscated their boots as evidence in the assault. The officers then escorted the complaining skinheads to the door and released them into the rainy night in their stocking feet.

Cutting Devices

Knives are common, though sheathed knives are not, probably because they extend too far below the flight jackets and could be seen easily by the police. Folding knifes are popular since they can be concealed in snug jean pockets or in the top of a tight boot. Walking canes have become popular recently. Canes are legal, of course, but some offer the added feature of a handle that when twisted unsheathes a razor-sharp blade.

Check the top of the boot for knives. Folded knives and unsheathed fixed blades are frequently carried in the boot for easy access.

Some cutting devices are decorated in Nazi symbols. Knife handles often bear a swastika or the German Iron Cross. Usually the symbols are added on by the skins, but occasionally you will see a knife or sword that is a genuine antique, either stolen or purchased at a knife show.

Molotov Cocktails

Skinheads like to use Molotov cocktails because, as with baseball bats, they are inexpensive, but nonetheless effective. They have been used to intimidate victims into not filing a complaint and against witnesses to frighten them into not testifying. Sometimes they are used against each other during intergang street brawls or to commit murder.

> An old, rambling frame house in a historic section of Salem, Oregon, was firebombed by four racist skinheads. Earlier in the day, skinheads had argued with occupants of the house; then, at 3:30 A.M., the suspects returned and threw a Molotov cocktail through the basement window, killing a black woman and a homosexual white man.

Firearms

As mentioned, the average street-level skinhead doesn't have the same fascination with firepower as other street gangs do. Even if skins were as fascinated, they generally do not have the money to buy them. It's for the latter reason that police officers are going to run into more bats and clubs than automatic weapons. Still there are guns out there, and always there are rumors of more.

Other gangs usually obtain guns by first getting money through robberies, car prowling, and home burglaries. However, several years ago a hard-core skin proudly proclaimed, "Skinheads don't do robberies and burglaries. Niggers do that stuff. We just want to spread our beliefs." Well, that may be true with some skinheads, but remember that there are many levels and many different factions now. And times change.

As the skinhead/white supremacy movement grows, more and more diverse people become involved, including robbers and burglars who are also racists. There have been cases where white supremacists have bought and sold firearms with drug dealers. The hard-core skins may be against drugs and dealers, especially black dealers, but it's a case of the end justifying the means. As a result, there are more guns among the ranks of street-level skinheads now than ever before.

That's the bad news. The good news is that most of the time skinheads are not dumb enough to carry guns on their person when they are hanging out on the corner dressed in their full regalia and are easily seen by the police. However, they do carry them in their cars and almost always keep them handy in their apartments and houses.

Officers should be especially cautious at rallies and events on private property. Skinheads' courage to carry weapons increases with their numbers and when they believe they are in a position of power.

> Police were called to break up a brawl at an Adolf Hitler birthday party attended by skinheads. Officers found two semiauto assault rifles, a semiautomatic handgun, and a large quantity of ammunition.
>
> •
>
> Five members of a neo-Nazi skinhead gang were arrested in Naples, Idaho, as they attempted to reach white supremacist Randy Weaver who was in a standoff with federal authorities. When the skinheads were stopped, several military-style weapons were found in their vehicle.
>
> •
>
> In Sacramento a skinhead was arrested for firing a gun at a group of blacks in a restaurant. When the police searched his vehicle they found an Uzi.
>
> •
>
> While dozens of skinheads and other white supremacists gathered on a farm in Oklahoma to

This shooting target was found in a skinhead's apartment.

hear several White Power bands, skins dressed in camouflage clothing and armed with assault weapons patrolled the perimeter.

Skinheads who hang out on street corners and in coffee shops are at the lowest level in the movement. They have limited or no contact with upper-echelon white supremacists, and as a result, their access to the more sophisticated weaponry is somewhat limited. However, you should never underestimate any of them.

Other skinheads, because of their positions or contacts with racist groups, are in a better position to come into contact with firearms, specifically military types.

A simultaneous ATF raid in Columbus, Georgia, and Birmingham, Alabama, not only resulted in the arrest of several skinheads, but netted 50 stolen M16 barrels, a pound of military explosives, a large quantity of ammunition, and four machine guns. Three Fort Benning soldiers are suspected of working with Birmingham skinhead leaders.

These and other similar seizures lead many authorities to believe white supremacists across the country are stockpiling weapons, most likely in preparation for their long-awaited race war. Although such a confrontation has been discussed among followers for years, and seems to be a dangling carrot that keeps everyone going, more and more weaponry among the upper echelon should be of concern to all law enforcement.

Some white supremacists viewed the Los Angeles riots, which occurred after the acquittal of four police officers accused of beating Rodney King, as just the beginning of the great white-black race war. Among many authorities in law enforcement, there is agreement that the riots sparked a new urgency among white supremacists to stockpile weapons.

Antiracist skinheads have access to all the same crude weapons as the racists, but they have firearms too. They may have access to even greater firepower if they have aligned themselves with left-wing activists, zealots who are not afraid to hurt people to save the world from evil.

The Military as a Source

The military has always been the perfect place for extremists to get training. Many militant blacks serving in the U.S. Army in the late 1960s said they were glad to be in the service, especially in Vietnam. They were happy to get the training and the easy access to weapons that could be stolen and sent home to be used later in the anticipated race war between blacks and whites.

Today, white supremacists are using the army, air force, navy, and National Guard for the same thing. Military personnel are recruited by white supremacists organizations and used to steal weapons for their expected race war.

> United States servicemen and women fighting in Saudi Arabia during Operation Desert Shield were sent anti-Semitic, racist letters from a skinhead organization in Nevada. The letters spoke of the "Jewish control of America" and warned that if Aryan soldiers died fighting a war for the Jews in Israel, then white women back home would marry nonwhites.
>
> •
>
> More than 500 weapons were found by police in the home of a technical sergeant with the Air National Guard in Massachusetts. Neo-Nazi paraphernalia was found along with 50,000 rounds of ammunition, a mortar, antitank gun, machine gun, and rocket launcher.

Indeed, the military is fertile ground for white supremacist organizations where young, impressionable recruits have easy access to sophisticated weapons. It's known that some hate groups even send people into the service just for the training. Even when a skinhead joins the service with no ulterior motive, his hate philosophy goes with him to a place he quickly discovers has many opportunities.

In 1985, members of the now-defunct White Patriot Party befriended soldiers at Fort Bragg, North Carolina. The White Patriots not only got them to steal weapons—shoulder-fired antitank rockets, claymore mines, LAW rockets, C-4 explosives, riot grenades, and a myriad of firearms—but had the soldiers train the Party followers in their use.

An army report estimates that 20 percent of stolen military hardware ends up in the hands of right-wingers. Although the military claims it has tightened up its security, recent arrests where large caches of stolen military weapons have been recovered indicate that security measures need to be tightened to an even greater level.

It's common for police officers to receive intelligence information that a local skinhead gang possesses military weapons, such as a case of hand grenades or a crate of M16s. Most of the time this information is false, usually the invention of a snitch trying to sound important. On the other hand, there are times when the information is good. The investigating officer, therefore, needs to follow up on all such tips.

Some authorities are concerned that white supremacists are stockpiling weapons at a time when some factions in the movement are advocating greater militancy. While most groups have talked cryptically about having the capability of fighting a race war if it were to start today, not one of them has revealed any details of their weapon caches.

On the surface, right-wing paramilitary training, after being overtly active in the 1980s, seems to be on the decline. However, there are some authorities who believe groups of racist extremists are still training, but have just taken their activity deeper underground. The rumors are not only about large, sophisticated, upper-echelon training camps, but also about small numbers of skinheads playing war games in forests and on beaches. It's not uncommon to find skinheads in possession of literature on military tactics and weaponry.

One thing's for sure: the acquisition and stockpiling of military weapons is still occurring at all levels of the movement.

CHAPTER 4

Racist skinheads hate just about everyone. Hate is their passion, it identifies them; it's their reason to exist. Antiracist skinheads also hate, although their hate is more focused toward law enforcement and racist skinheads. It's important that you always consider both skinhead factions a threat to police officers and to all elements of the general public.

POLICE OFFICERS

Let's begin with the target most important to you: you. As a member of the law enforcement community, you automatically are hated and distrusted by both the racists and antiracists. To the racists, you are part of ZOG, the Jewish controlled government that dictates and controls everything you do. To the antiracists, you are a racist, head-thumping oppressor who most likely sympathizes with the racist skins.

As silly as the concept of ZOG is, racist skinheads believe it. Their intense conviction of its truth makes them distrust you since you are the muscle behind the Jewish conspiracy to oppress the white working man. Believing this makes them paranoid. They see a police officer and an FBI agent behind every bush and telephone pole. They are convinced they are under

SKINHEAD HATE TARGETS

TO PROTECT AND SERVE
THE ZIONIST INTERNATIONAL

You, "Boys in Blue,"
Who serve the Jew . . .
Think you're making things safe,
but they're just pimping you.

They throw you bones,
and protect their vile skins . . .
Splitting on your own kinsmen,
again and again.

Now, there's WAR in the air,
because we've had enough . . .
And real damn soon,
it's gonna get rough!

Righteous WHITE anger,
is what you will feel . . .
As we smash the system,
with fire and steel!

Your Jew masters we'll pile,
on Huge smoking pyres . . .
YOUR ASS IS OURS!!

—An anonymous skinhead

constant surveillance and that their phones are continuously being tapped. Indeed, white supremacists of all levels, and antiracists for that matter, are the most suspicious group you will ever encounter.

Antiracist skinheads are under the impression they have carte blanche to use any means they choose to eradicate neo-Nazi, racist skinheads. Since your job is to stop them from committing crimes on other skins and to arrest them when they do break the law, you are seen as an obstacle, another enemy with whom they have to deal.

Officers of color *generally* do not have a problem when they are partnered with a white officer and dealing only with two or three racist skinheads. But when there are fewer officers than skinheads, or just one minority officer working alone, the potential for problems increases. Officers of all colors, including white, report that they have been assaulted and called "nigger" and "Jew puppets" with no other apparent motive than that they were wearing uniforms and thus representing ZOG.

If you actively work skinheads, it's possible—in fact it's likely—that you specifically will become a target of their hate. You may find your name mentioned in their literature and on their telephone hate lines. You may even discover that your name has been placed on a skinhead hit list.

The normal precautions that most law enforcement officers take are more important than ever.

- Use your work address when you register your personal car
- Use your work address on your personal checks
- Do not list your home telephone number
- Instruct your high-school-age children not to tell their friends that you work skinheads
- Always be cautious of your surroundings, on and off duty

Is this being paranoid? No. My family has been followed, my name has been on a hit list, my kids have been watched, I have been sent hate literature, my name has been chanted at demonstrations, I have been recognized numerous times off duty, and even the county library computer was tapped to use my library card number to order all kinds of books on racism.

It's paramount to keep in mind that if someone wants

Many skinhead graffiti messages are anti-Semitic.

to find you, it takes little effort to learn where you live and just about any other pertinent information about you. You need to stay alert and exercise every precaution to protect yourself and your family.

> An officer in Utah had a take-home police car, which he parked alongside his house. One day while he was inside his home, his police car was firebombed, and white supremacy literature was found scattered about his yard.

JEWS

Across the board, racist skinheads and all white supremacists hate the Jews. It can be alarming to see a 14-year-old skinhead's face twist into an ugly mask at the mention of the word Jew. His eyes harden and his mouth tightens as if he were tasting something bitter, as he spits, "Those fucking Jew bastards are destroying everything. We want to kill them all."

As one piece of literature says:

> We oppose the capitalist and the communist scum that are destroying the Aryan race. We realize that the parasitic Jewish race is at the heart of our problem.

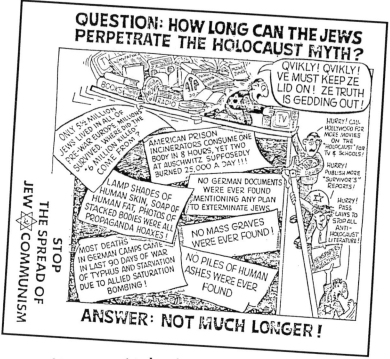

*Most white supremacists do not
believe the Holocaust occurred.*

An "informed" skinhead can go on and on about
how the international Jewish conspiracy has fabricated
the lie about six million people dying in Hitler's
Holocaust and how Anne Frank's diary of her World
War II experiences was a Jewish forgery. Just about
everything that has gone wrong over the years, they
claim, is the work of Satan's Jews.

A white supremacist behind bars wrote the following:

> At the time the Jews took over our monetary
> system via the Federal Reserve and instituted the
> income tax in 1913, the White Race constituted
> about 40 percent of the Earth's population. Since
> then, the Jews have instigated two World Wars
> and the Russian Revolution. These three events
> alone resulted in the death of over 80 million

White Christians, most of them being young males and the genetic cream of our race.

Next, they laid such heavy taxes on the white workers of the world that it became, if not impossible, very financially impractical to have children. At the same time, the Jews took the taxes stolen from the labor of productive Whites and gave it the non-whites, both here and abroad, encouraging them to have from 10-20 children. They used their media to insult and emasculate the White man while depicting non-white males to be heroes so white women would desert their race by the millions.

The result is that the percentage of child-bearing women in the world today who are White and married to White men is at best four percent. Add to this the fact that we have no nation or territorial imperative of our own where we can propagate, promote, and protect our own kind, and you can begin to see what a hill we have to climb if we are to preserve our existence as a race.

Although the Jews have always been hated by racist skinheads, it seems their abhorrence for all that is Jewish and everything that is perceived as Jewish began to intensify around early 1990 and has continued to the present. Perhaps skinheads blame the Jews for the recession and their inability to get jobs. Although the impetus for the upswing has not been examined, anti-Semitic rhetoric, graffiti on synagogues, and harassing and threatening phone calls to Jewish businesses and organizations have increased at an alarming rate.

BLACKS

According to the Christian Identity faith, blacks are part of the mud race, a mistake that God made when he was creating the world. Since they are a mistake, they do not count because they are not human. As one white supremacist bluntly explained, "Killing a nigger is no different than killing a dog."

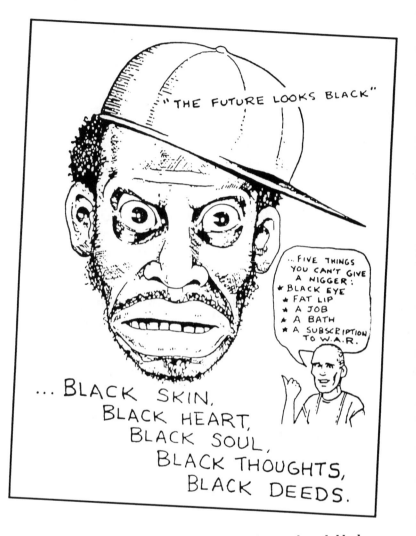

This flier is typical of the ones skinheads distribute to degrade blacks.

Racist skinheads blame much of the United States' drug problems on blacks. Tom Metzger's *WAR* newspaper frequently displays cartoons of black people with exaggerated physical features, dress style, and speech patterns, usually in some kind of a predicament involving drugs.

Racist skinheads use every stereotype imaginable to

perpetuate a negative image of the black experience. This does much to boost the self-esteem of white racist skins while keeping alive the belief that blacks are inferior and less than human.

Black people have been attacked by skinheads across the country for no other reason than their being black.

Hillsboro, Oregon: Two racist skinheads fired shots into a car containing two black men.

Granada Hills, California: Four skinheads shouting racial slurs chased a black pizza delivery man in their vehicle, then struck him with a piece of asphalt.

Arlington Heights, Illinois: Several skinheads were charged for attacking a black police cadet.

Las Vegas, Nevada: Two white supremacists were arrested for beating an interracial couple.

Port Richmond, New York: Four skinheads with clubs beat a black man.

Birmingham, Alabama: A skinhead shot a black youth in the back.

Arlington, Texas: Three white supremacists teenagers murdered a black man in a drive-by shooting. The victim had been picked at random.

Skinheads complain that although there is a Black Miss America contest, black awards festivities, and a Black Entertainment Network, no one has ever filed a discrimination suit, including the American Civil Liberties Union (ACLU).

A White Entertainment Network, they say, is unthinkable.

OTHER PEOPLE OF COLOR

Klanwatch, a monthly intelligence report published by the Southern Poverty Law Center, reports that Asians, Hispanics, and other people of color are victimized every month across the United States. When a racist skinhead sees a person of color, the target is easily identifiable and instantly dehumanized. This process is similar to the way in which soldiers dehumanize the enemy by calling them gooks, nips, krauts, and, most recently, ragheads. When the enemy looks different and is thought of as less than human, it's much easier to criticize, hurt, and kill him.

> The three skinheads noticed the Korean man as he was leaving a restaurant. They began chanting, "Gook! Gook!" and shouted at him to "get back to Korea" and "get out of our country!" When the Oriental man stood his ground, he was struck repeatedly by the skinheads, knocked to the ground, and kicked over and over by their heavy Doc Marten boots. Before they fled, they called him names again and spit on his face.

•

> Several racist skinheads approached a Hispanic boy as he sat on a bench in the shopping mall waiting for his mother. They called him several racial epithets and then banged his head several times into the bench before they ran off.

MIXED-RACE COUPLES

According to a government study made in 1993, one out of every 50 marriages in the United States is biracial. In 1992 alone, there were 246,000 black-white couples, nearly four times the number in 1970. Additionally, 883,000 other marriages occurred between whites and other races, such as Asians, Native Americans, and Pacific Islanders. These statistics represent only those couples who have married, not the thousands who are living together.

A skinhead poster showing their disgust with interracial couples.

Skinheads hate this. In fact, all white supremacists despise racial mixing, believing it's just another Jewish conspiracy against Christians, in particular white Christians. White supremacists believe that the children of mixed-race couples muddy the race.

When white people have romantic relationships with

minorites, they are considered "traitors to the white race"—and worse when they marry. Attacks on mixed-race couples are commonplace, which almost always involve both parties being assaulted, with the white person most often receiving the brunt of the beating.

> During the three months a mixed-race couple had lived in their Lake City, Florida, home, they were the victims of more than 20 incidents of harassment and vandalism. Passersby shouted racial slurs from their cars, and vandals sprayed "nigger" and "white trash" on the couple's home and scratched "KKK" into their car. The family subsequently moved away.
>
> •
>
> A white man and his Hispanic girlfriend were sitting in their car in an area known as a lover's lane. A white van pulled up behind them, and several skinheads scrambled out and surrounded the lovers' car. They pulled the couple out and beat them with long, steel flashlights, the type carried by police officers. Then, shouting racial epithets at the woman and "race traitor" at the man, the skinheads executed a boot party, before pushing the couple over an embankment.

The couple does not have to be male and female. Mixed-race couples of the same sex, not necessarily gay, also get attacked. Racist skinheads do not like the idea of whites even fraternizing with people from other races.

> Two young boys, one black, the other white, were shooting baskets on the grade school playground. Three skinheads ran onto the court, grabbed the boys' skateboards and commenced beating the two with them, shouting, "No race mixing! No race mixing!"

GAYS

The epidemic of HIV and the AIDS virus in the gay community makes them an easy target for the skins to hate. Although skinheads frequently attack gays, their concern about getting spattered with AIDS-infected blood has probably kept the number of assaults lower than what it might otherwise be.

Skinheads hate gays because their relationships do not perpetuate the white race. White supremacists are taught through their literature that gay sex is as wrong as race mixing, since neither helps the white population at this critical time when it's declining worldwide.

White supremacists' image of the ideal white man is one who is God-fearing, virile, and muscular, standing tall and proud with his white, fertile woman at his side. With this picture in the forefront of their minds, white supremacists have suggested through their literature that, with so many effeminate men around, white women are going to seek out masculine black men as sex partners.

> A skinhead was asked if the beating death of a gay man in New York by racist skinheads served the white supremacists' cause. "Oh, it can get you into a lot of trouble. But a lot of people look at it as a way to clean up the streets—as war—as one less fag to take care of . . . I don't see it as wrong . . . Fuck those fucking people—they're nothing. They fucking breathe my air. They're just against everything I believe in."
>
> •
>
> A gay man was carrying two video movies as he left an adult bookstore that sold only gay videos and books. Two skinheads ran up to him, beat him to the sidewalk, booted him, then ran off with his movies.

WHITES

Many people are confused by the fact that whites are victimized far more than minorities by racist skinheads. When the skinhead problem began in Portland, white people were harassed, intimidated, menaced, and assaulted twice as often as blacks, Asians, and gay people. The victims were not other gang members, but mall shoppers, people taking a walk, drivers stopped at a red light. Regular people, very young to very old.

With fliers like this one, skinheads hope to get all whites to think the same way they do.

How does this make sense? Why would white, racist skinheads who believe that white is right and all other races are mud people attack other whites? The answer is clear: racist skinhead gangs consist of thugs, bullies, cowards, and violent individuals who, when on the prowl to hurt someone, pick the first weak person they see. And since the majority of people in most cities is white, there are naturally more whites available to attack.

Many assaults are preceded by heavy beer drinking in an apartment or park. Once the skins' courage is fortified with drink, they begin looking for a hapless victim. Their prowling might begin on foot, stomping along the sidewalk, five to 10 strong, or they might all load into a van or into two or three cars. When they select a victim, and it's usually someone alone, they will either attack without provocation or in some way bait the person. For example, they might ask a male, "What do you think of white power?" A female: "Do you ever date niggers?" The people asked these questions can give no right answer to these questions since the skins have already made up their minds to harass or assault them.

Scenes like these are repeated all too frequently around the country. Although most attacks are executed without much thought or planning and carried out simply for the pure enjoyment of it, there is in some cases a philosophy behind the action. Some racist skinheads believe that "if you are not with us, then you are part of the problem." In their minds, whites who do not stand up and fight for the rights of the white man are no better than the muds.

MISTAKEN IDENTITIES

It's not uncommon for people to be attacked by racist skinheads because they are perceived to be gay or of some minority when, in fact, they are not. Straight people have been attacked as they walked by a gay bar or as they were crossing the street in an area frequented by gays. Dark-complected people have been harassed and assaulted by skinheads because they were thought to be East Indian or Hispanic.

Antiracist skinheads have made mistakes as well. During periods of heightened antiracist activity, there have been incidents where people have been victimized because the antiracist skins thought they were racists or that they associated with the neo-Nazis.

ZIONIST OCCUPATIONAL GOVERNMENT (ZOG)

Zionist: Someone who will sacrifice any person, anything, or any nation for the greater good of Israel.

Occupational: Possession by force, rather than by voluntary agreement.

Government: Control of a population.

Skinheads and white supremacists believe if you take the time to look for ZOG, you will soon be knee-deep in evidence that supports its existence. If you ask skinheads about the media, they will rattle off a list of Jewish-sounding names they believe control the news on television and radio and in the newspapers. They will quote people who have made comments that support their beliefs. For example, Charles A. Lindbergh is quoted as

Skinheads believe that the "system" is controlled by Jews, otherwise know as the Zionist Occupational Government.

writing in his wartime journals, "We are disturbed about the effect of the Jewish influence on our press, radio, and motion pictures. It may become very serious." Newsman Tom Brokaw supposedly replied to Jews who asked him whose side of the American media he was on, "You have nothing to worry about."

White supremacists talk of the injustice of the Jewish-controlled justice system. They complain that although Jews want to be considered Caucasian in every respect, they also want, and now get, protection under the civil rights laws originally passed to protect non-Caucasians.

They claim that the FBI exercises creative reporting, citing an annual report that omitted the firebombing of the Institute of Historical Review (an organization that believes the Holocaust was a hoax). White supremacists do acknowledge that FBI reports showed that Jewish extremists accounted for four violent incidents, two murders, and nine injuries. But then they are quick to complain that not one Jewish suspect has been brought to justice for these actions. They also cite incidents where Jews have been given six or seven months in jail for their violent, revolutionary activities, whereas white supremacists have been given 150 years for their crimes.

They believe that Jews control the entertainment industry and cite support in their beliefs from notable people. Author Truman Capote is said to have assailed what he called the "Jewish Mafia" for monopolizing U.S. publishing and suppressing writings that did not meet with Jewish approval. Marlon Brando is quoted as saying in *Playboy* magazine, "You've seen every race besmirched, but you never saw an unfavorable image of a kike because the Jews are ever watchful for that. They never allow it to be shown on the screen."

Skinheads are concerned about the growing political power of the Jews. They use a quote from 1935 edition of the *Jewish Daily Bulletin*: "There is only one power which really counts: The power of political pressure. We Jews are the most powerful people on earth because we have this power, and we know how to apply it."

Fliers such as this show how skinheads feel about Jewish people.

White supremacists say that an American Jewish Committee poll in 1982 found that 75 percent of all American Jews openly admitted a devotion to Israel that superseded their allegiance to the United States. They claim that countless American politicians who have refused to become puppets have been targeted by Zionists for defeat, including

Congressmen Findley and McClosky, Senators Joe McCarthy and Charles Percy, presidential hopefuls like John Connally (former governor of Texas) and black civil rights leader and politician Jesse Jackson, and even presidents in office. From C.C. O'Brien's *The Siege,* they quote: "President Ford made known his displeasure with Israel—something he was to regret the following year [1976]."

The bottom line is that the Jews are hated by all white supremacists, an emotion that is often the motive behind skinhead activities and crimes, as this flier illustrates:

> The problem goes back to time memorial. Good versus evil. Satan versus God. Call them what you may, there has always been a race of the evil seed around to plague us. Eventually they worm their way into the uppermost seats of the church and government, then there goes the neighborhood. Say hello to high interest rates (usury), prostitution, immorality, and every other vice known to mankind. And they love every minute of it as they enslave humanity and laugh all the way to the bank. These wonderful little hooked nosed parasites have been kicked out of every nation in Europe at one time or another for their treasonous acts. They were not allowed to vote or to hold property in the colonies for many years until some liberals gave in and decided it would probably be alright and couldn't hurt anyone. What a mistake. Our fathers knew of their treacherous spirits and knew to keep them at arm's length . . .
>
> There was one man who understood the problems and met them head on. This man was Adolph Hitler, loved by the people as none other was. Maybe this could be the salvation for the people from the clutches of the oppressors. No, the international banking community would never permit this. They couldn't lose control of the masses they had enslaved. They had to rally the world against the truth of the good German people. The people and leaders must be crushed and enslaved forever.

CHAPTER 5

I f you have been in law enforcement for more than a year or two, you know there are no limits to how low some people will sink to get attention or to take advantage of others. Falsifying hate crimes is no exception. In fact, false reports by people claiming to be victims of hate crimes are on the rise.

Hate crimes are big news. A cross burning, a racially motivated assault, get headlines. When people read about it in the newspapers they are shocked, angry, they have a sudden feeling of helplessness, and they feel a strong need to do something. They want to help the victims, usually with moral support, food, gifts, and money. This in turn gets more media attention, which results in even more community help.

That is why so many people are affected when it turns out a hate crime is really a hoax, an event fabricated for the attention it gets the "victim"or for the material goods that are donated by a distressed community. The concerned, giving people are embarrassed; they feel stupid and used. The investigating police agency has wasted time, precious manpower, and money on a staged crime, while real crimes are still occurring. And the people who staged the hate crime get arrested for falsifying a police report. If they choose not to move away, their neighbors' angry stares make life miserable for them.

A black woman who was confined to a wheelchair and a white woman with whom she was living staged 20 hate crimes over a period of several months. The crimes included cross burnings, hate mail, death threats, and graffiti, all directed at the black woman's race. The police department spent over $30,000 investigating the crimes, and hundreds of people in the community held marches and rallies, patrolled, staked out the neighborhood, and even used their own money to buy surveillance equipment.

The police eventually determined the women had created all of the crimes themselves and arrested them. It was even discovered that the wheelchair-bound woman could really walk. The police held a press conference the day after the "victim's" neighborhood had conducted a large march and rally against racism.

The information shocked and confused everyone, especially activists who were fighting hard against hate crimes.

A week later, the black woman attempted suicide, and the white woman moved out of the city.

Sometimes law enforcement officers are suspicious of the validity of a claim but are hesitant to mention their concerns for fear of being called racist or homophobic.

A 27-year-old female minister with San Francisco's Metropolitan Community Church made two claims that she had been the victim of homophobic attacks. In the first attack, she said she had been struck in the face with a shovel by someone who had broken into her home. She also said someone had painted the words "Die with Your Fags" on the wall. Then two weeks later, she reported that she was pulled into a car by two skinheads who assaulted her and threatened to kill her because she was a lesbian and worked with AIDS victims. Later in the investigation, she claimed she had been raped by the skinheads.

Subsequently the claims were all found to be fabricated. The police later said they had doubted her story from the beginning because her wounds appeared self-inflicted and her delayed claim of rape was suspicious. The officers had been afraid to voice their suspicions, however, because they knew they would be accused of being insensitive to homosexuals.

Before her hoax was made public, the police chief formed a task force to investigate attacks against homosexuals, the mayor offered an award of $10,000 for information leading to the attackers' arrest, and hundreds of people held a sit-down strike to protest her assault.

She subsequently resigned her pastorship and fled to the midwest, never receiving her punishment and leaving the San Francisco gay community with a large credibility problem.

Even more important, however, is the effect of the hoax on the struggle to combat hate crimes. Once a hoax has been discovered, then reported as such in the media, everyone—press, public, and the police—looks at hate crime complaints with a skeptical eye.

The home of a black couple living in an all-white neighborhood was burned to the ground just two weeks after it was ransacked and covered with swastikas. Immediately, neighbors and strangers brought food, clothing, and supplies to the family.

But public outpouring of sympathy changed quickly when it was discovered the crimes were not committed by skinheads but by the black family. A counselor with the Veteran's Administration spoke for many when he said, "It sort of dilutes my faith in humanity because I was prepared to make a sacrifice on their behalf."

The skepticism that occurs after a falsified hate crime has been uncovered does much to undermine the efforts of people who actively fight racism and hate violence. It's difficult for activists to get others to support their cause when there is a possibility the effort might come back and slap them in the face. Additionally, the prevailing skepticism doubly victimizes the real victims of hate crimes because the pressure is on them to prove the validity of their claims.

Sometimes charlatans are easy to detect, usually because of their ignorance of the particulars of a hate crime or because they are unaware of the knowledge the police have. For example, as already mentioned, skinheads know how to draw a swastika and make other forms of white supremacy graffiti. However, many hoaxes involve graffiti that are done inaccurately, such as backward swastikas and incorrectly phrased white supremacy slogans.

Staged cross burnings often follow real ones. If a cross burning garners a lot of publicity and concerned citizens give money and goods to the victim family, it's almost a guarantee there will be another cross burning within a few days.

Another indicator of a hoax is when the "victims" are too careful when staging their scene.

> The Jewish owner of a restaurant filed a report of vandalism. Officers found swastikas on the walls and furnishings in disarray. At first glance the officers thought they really had a hate crime. But upon closer examination, the officers noted that the disarray appeared too neat. Dishes were scattered about, but none were broken. A television had been unscrewed from its cable then laid gently on its side.

The majority of hate crimes are real, and the terror the victims experience is real. You need to keep in mind, however, that charlatans and opportunists abound.

CHAPTER 6

We have a new set of targets to play with. So if you are white and work for the system, watch your step. Whether you be a system cop, a controlled judge, or a crooked lawyer, your ass is grass.
—Tom Metzger, 1990

I first spoke with WAR's founder, Tom Metzger, in late 1989. I had been working skinheads for two years at that time, and it occurred to me that maybe I should talk to the big man himself. In those days, everything was Tom Metzger this and Tom Metzger that. I decided that if I was going to be completely well-rounded in this business, I should at least introduce myself.

So I called him at home, and damned if he didn't answer. I must admit I was a little anxious initially, but two minutes into the call we were chatting like old friends. Well, maybe that is overstating it a little, but at least we were talking.

I told him who I was and what I did in the GET. He said he was familiar with me from videotapes of newscast about skinheads sent to him by his Portland people.

At first, he said he didn't want to talk to me since I might testify against him at his then upcoming civil trial. Nonetheless he went on to talk for 30 minutes, chatting about several things going on in the movement and what was happen-

THIS IS WAR

ing with his case. When I asked if he had received any threats regarding the trial, he told me of a recent incident where a high-powered arrow was fired through his front window and into the wall two feet above his easy chair. When I asked if this scared him, since he had small children, he verbally shrugged it off with, "No, I just hung a pair of wet socks over it to dry."

He was personable on the phone, easy to talk to, and up front about his beliefs. This initial conversation helped to set the foundation for a working relationship that facilitated the monstrous work that would go into his trial nine months later.

WHO IS TOM METZGER?

Tom Metzger, now in his mid-50s, shows no sign of slowing down. In fact, he seems more active now than ever. So who is this man, where did he come from, and how did he become a mentor of racist skinheads? Let's take a brief look at the chronology of his past 30 years.

1960s
Tom Metzger got his start in organized white supremacy in the John Birch Society, a fiercely anti-Communist, right-wing organization. He also joined the Minutemen, a right-wing paramilitary organization that stockpiled weapons and trained members in guerrilla war tactics.

1970s
He quit the John Birch Society in the early 1970s purportedly because they didn't promote breaking the law by refusing to pay taxes. In 1975 he became a minister in James Warner's New Christian Crusade church, a branch of Christian Identity. He has since dropped Christian Identity, although he still maintains ties with some of its adherents. Also around this time, Metzger joined the Knights of the Ku Klux Klan, led by David Duke, who was steering the Klan toward neo-Nazism. Metzger went on to be the leader of the Klan in California, gaining noto-

*Tom Metzger's White Student Union
was depicted in posters such as this.*

riety by organizing a border patrol to prevent illegal aliens from entering the United States.

1980s

In 1980, Metzger ran for the Democratic Party nomination of California's 45th Congressional District. He garnered more than 33,000 votes but lost the general election. In 1982, he got more than 75,000 votes statewide in the race for the Democratic nomination for the U.S. Senate. In the mid-1980s, Metzger formed White Aryan Resistance, WAR, which he continues to lead. In his first *WAR* newspaper, he wrote that WAR "will not walk a conservative line," that "it is neither left nor right. Whatever benefits the white racial culture, we endorse. Whatever degrades our race, we oppose." In 1987, Tom Metzger's son, John, assumed the leadership role of Aryan Youth Movement/White Student Union, which was originally founded in 1984. Subsequently, John changed the name to WAR Youth.

1990

After two weeks of testimony from dozens of witnesses, Tom and John Metzger were found guilty in a civil suit in Portland of being responsible for sending agents there to indoctrinate skinheads and incite them to violence, ultimately causing the beating death of an Ethiopian man. The lawsuit awarded the victim's family $12.5 million.

Prior to the trial in October 1990, Tom Metzger made several trips to Portland to file motions. On each visit he would hold press interviews to draw attention to himself in hopes of getting donations to his organization to help finance his defense. On one visit, he informed the press that he was going to a radio station where, during an earlier visit, he had been a guest on a talk show hosted by a blind black man, a man Metzger claimed he liked. The station had recently received a lot of press because of a burglary where the suspect, who turned out to be a recently fired employee, had marked the inside walls

Working For White America
Through The Advancement And
Enhancement of Aryan Youth.

WHITE STUDENT UNION
Every Other Group Has Representation
Why Not Us?

HOLLYWOOD, FL. 33081   FALLBROOK, CA 92028

The business card of a Florida
White Student Union chapter.

with large swastikas. When Metzger arrived at the station, he made a show of offering his condolences to his black friend with a big hug and a check for $150.

As the trial date approached, we were receiving continual intelligence of doom and gloom, in the form of skinhead attacks on the courthouse and bombings of the courtroom. In fact, a bomb was exploded in a courthouse in San Diego with a warning to stop the Portland trial. This added to our concerns, resulting in virtually everyone involved with the trial getting police protection.

Since Tom Metzger and his son were despised by the majority of people, they received most of the death threats. Regardless of their detestable, racist philosophy, we could not let them get hurt in our city. Since I had developed a working relationship with him during his previous visits, I was assigned to set up his protection and be responsible for getting him to and from the courthouse each day.

Planning for Metzger's security began with a series of telephone calls to him. He was open to our plan, probably because of his own concerns after the bombing, and because of all the threats he had been getting on his message lines. The planning bogged down when the judge said Metzger would not be able to have seven of his own people, who were acting as personal bodyguards, sit with him in the courtroom. Later, however, the judge agreed to Metzger's request, either because it wasn't that unreasonable, considering that the plaintiff's attorney's had a dozen or more aids, or because Metzger threatened that if he would not be allowed to bring in his people, he and his son would refuse all police protection and simply walk down the street to the courthouse. Given the rage Portlanders were feeling at that time, this would have caused a riot. Fortunately, we did not have to deal with that.

On the Sunday evening before the first day of trial, Metzger called to tell me that he and his entourage had arrived and were staying in a hotel outside of town. I told him my partner and I would be there in an hour to go over the last-minute changes in security.

An hour later, we were standing outside his door waiting for someone to answer our knock. It seemed like minutes passed before a muffled voice from the other side asked, "Who's there?" I gave our names, and we were left waiting another minute. Then the door opened an inch, and a set of eyes peered out. The door closed, and we waited another minute before it opened again, this time just wide enough to let us slip by.

I nodded at the hard-looking young man holding the door, a face I recognized from photos given me by an informant. I had been told he was a boxer, and he definitely had a face that had forgotten to duck a few hard jabs.

Six pairs of eyes watched us carefully as we moved into the small, hot room. The air was thick with smoke and suspicion. John Metzger was sitting on a twin bed in his boxers and a T-shirt, holding a beer; Tom, wearing a strap T-shirt and slacks, was sitting on the edge of the other bed, also nursing a beer. The others were sitting on the floor or in chairs, drinking and puffing nervously on cigarettes.

Tom stood and responded to my extended hand with a surprisingly warm handshake and a smile. I introduced

This photo was taken during the Metzgers' civil trial in 1990 in Portland. From left to right: John Metzger, son of Tom Metzger; the author, Loren Christensen; and Tom Metzger, founder of WAR.

my partner, and Tom introduced his people, all of whom nodded with tight reserve. Although I had not met them before, I recognized most of them from advanced intelligence information. It was a strained moment, to say the least, and I knew if something wasn't done to break the ice it was going to be a long two weeks.

Although I already knew the answer, I asked which of them had punched out Geraldo Rivera and broke his nose, referring to the incident that had happened on Geraldo's show a few months earlier. The big guy sitting next to me snapped his hand up as eagerly as a second grader wanting recognition for a job well done and shouted, "I did! That was me."

I faked a laugh, leaned toward him, and playfully slapped him on the shoulder. "I just want to shake your hand," I said, pumping it with phony enthusiasm. "Job well done."

The room immediately exploded into laughter, pulls were taken from beers, and fresh cigarettes were lit. The ice had been broken.

Security for the trial was unprecedented for the entire two weeks. More than 100 uniform officers were assigned courthouse security and crowd control each day, including the bomb squad, detectives, and Special Emergency Reaction Team (SERT, a SWAT team) officers who were positioned on rooftops and on foot at the unloading point where all participants arrived. For the first few days, a helicopter, hovering just above the street, was used to monitor the arrival point.

Two of us rode in the van used to pick up the Metzgers and their entourage, and two officers rode in a follow car. We would use cryptic radio communication to make a quick arrival at the courthouse, where we would exit the van, move to a sidewalk elevator, then be lowered to a tunnel under the sidewalk. From there we would scurry to another elevator, which would take us up to the fifth-floor courtroom.

The jury, judge, and attorneys also used the same security measures. In addition to the officers in and around the courthouse, there was a squad of SERT officers and a squad of regular uniform officers in a nearby room.

My team maintained elbow-to-elbow security on the Metzgers during the entire two weeks. They never left the courthouse, taking their coffee and lunch breaks in an empty courtroom. Although we represented ZOG and all that that meant to the Metzgers, they cooperated completely with us and appeared grateful for the way we got them through it.

1991

In early 1991, San Diego authorities seized a skinhead meeting hall owned by Tom Metzger and the equipment he used to produce his *WAR* newspaper and cable TV show, "Race and Reason." But in May 1991, Metzger got one up on ZOG when he began collecting welfare, drawing $960 a month.

1992

What has to be one of Tom Metzger's worse years began with the seizure of his family home, forcing him to move into an apartment. Later in the year he went to jail for his involvement in a 1984 cross burning in California. After serving four months, he was released early to tend to his terminally ill wife, who passed away within a few days. Toward the end of the year, he was arrested in Canada for racial activities, then kicked out of the country a few days later.

In late 1992, I spoke with him in Salem, Oregon, where he was filing an appeal on his civil suit (which he lost six months later). Although his home and personal property had been seized, he claimed he had yet to pay a dime toward the lawsuit. He told reporters he was living in a nice apartment with a pool, drove a new car, and that his newspaper and TV show were bigger than ever.

I doubt that things are as rosy as he wants us to believe. When it was disclosed during the 1990 trial that he was pocketing some of the money his followers were contributing to his organization, many skinheads, feeling abused, turned their backs on him. Today, skinheads in the Northwest never mention his name.

But Metzger is a survivor. Just the fact that he is pretending that things are better than ever and wants it to appear that he is still active in his struggle is good reason for law enforcement to keep watching him. The white supremacy movement is in constant flux, and with the monstrous skinhead situation going on in Europe and the constant media attention on racism in this country, Metzger just may regain the leadership he once enjoyed.

Minutes after the jury returned with a $12.5 million judgment in his 1990 civil case, Tom and John met with a horde from the press. The Metzgers sat silently behind a table for a moment, appearing undaunted by the verdict. Tom's eyes narrowed as he slowly scanned the crowded, silent room. Then he spoke these chilling words:

"The movement will not be stopped in the puny town of Portland. We're too deep. We're embedded now. Don't you understand? We're in your colleges; we're in your armies; we're in your police forces; we're in your technical areas; we're in your banks. Where do you think a lot of these skinheads disappear to? We've planted the seeds. Stopping Tom Metzger is not gonna change what's going to happen to this country."

CHAPTER 7

Although you are probably more interested in reading about the kinds of weapons skinheads carry and the meaning of their tattoos, you also need to be aware of the material in this section. You do not need to be a theologian to work skinheads, but it's necessary to have some understanding of the religion many of them follow in order to have an insight into their thinking and the motivation behind their actions.

In a nutshell, Christian Identity is a fundamental Christian theology structured to support racism. It teaches that Jews are the children of Satan and that all races but Caucasian are the result of a mistake God made as he was creating the world.

Irwin Suall, fact-finding director of the Anti-Defamation League of B'nai B'rith of New York City says:

> "There are groups known as seed believers. They are the ones that hold that Jews are literally the offspring of the devil. Their term is 'the spawn of Satan.' There are others who are less extreme but still believe that the Jews are not the true biblical Israelites but are evil people."

What this means to people who

CHRISTIAN IDENTITY

believe in Christian Identity is that Jews and all people of color are inferior. It's this belief that gives skinheads and thousands of white supremacists the justification to feel superior, to hate, and to commit racial crimes.

As with all religions, different Christian Identity churches teach variations on the theme. For our purposes, let's just take a general look at the religion to get an impression of what it's about and how it motivates many of its followers.

TEACHINGS OF EDWARD HINE

Christian Identity was founded by Edward Hine, a Britisher, who in 1871 published a book called *Identification of the British Nation with Lost Israel*, a huge publishing success in its day. In the late 1800s, the book was brought to the United States by two of his followers and has since flourished. Below are a few of Hine's concepts.

The Real Jews

Since before the birth of Jesus, all the world has held an inaccurate understanding of who the true Jews are, Hines taught. The real Jews, the descendants of Moses, Abraham, and Jesus, whom God called his Chosen People, are the people of the British Isles. The others, those we have erroneously thought were the Jews, are actually a race of Mongolian-Turkish Khazars who descended from the seed Satan put into Eve's belly along with Adam's seed. Of the two sons bore by Eve, Abel was Adam's and Cain was Satan's. Cain murdered Abel, and later Cain's descendants murdered Jesus. Today, Christian Identity followers believe the Jews are still trying to kill all white Christians.

The Lost Tribes of Israel

A great amount of Identity literature concerns the Lost Tribes of Israel. Forming it all into something concise, readable, and applicable to law enforcement is difficult, but in a nutshell it goes like this:

Two thousand years before the birth of Jesus, Abraham and his wife were given a son, Isaac, who bore two sons, Jacob and Esau. Jacob took two wives and two concubines and had 12 sons, each of whom became head of one of the 12 tribes of Israel.

Jacob, who was not a Jew, changed his name to Israel, and thus we have the story of the Israelites and the 12 tribes of Israel. Identity believes these were not Jews, but rather only tribes of Israel. Soon thereafter, the 12 were placed in bondage by the rulers of Egypt and remained there for 430 years until Moses led them out.

Once the people had reached the promised land, God gave each tribe, except one, a portion of the land. God appointed the tribe of Levi to a priesthood and assigned it to serve the others. The land that Levi would have received went to Joseph's son, Manasseh, thus creating the legendary thirteenth tribe of Israel.

Over the next few hundred years in the Holy Land, the remaining tribes formed a northern and southern branch. The three tribes in the south became known as Judah, a word that is sometimes translated to mean Jews. Some Identity scholars say the northern tribes were conquered and never heard from again, while other writers believe they each formed countries, known today as Sweden, Denmark, Holland, and so on.

In 586 B.C., Babylonia captured the tribe of Judah, killed many of them, plundered the temple of Jerusalem, and took the survivors into captivity. Babylon was the kingdom of Cain, who had fled there after killing Abel. It was during those years in captivity, years of being exposed to the black magic of Satan, that the tribe of Judah became the worldwide, evil force it is today, according to Identity teachings.

Here is where the United States gets involved. Christian Identity teaches that the thirteenth tribe, Manasseh's, subsequently moved to Europe, then crossed the Atlantic on the *Mayflower* to America. Here they eventually received what they consider sacred documents, such as the Declaration of Independence, the

Constitution, and the first 10 amendments, known as the Bill of Rights. Identity believes that all subsequent amendments were dictated by Satan's Jewish forces to bring down the white race.

CURRENT TEACHINGS

Christian Identity captured the public's attention in 1983, when law enforcement agencies were looking for Gordon Kahl, a Posse Comitatus member who had shot and killed two federal marshals in North Dakota (in 1991, Kahl's life was depicted in a made-for-television movie). By the time Kahl was killed in a shoot-out in Arkansas, the press had educated the general public about Christian Identity and its link to violence-prone racist organizations.

In 1992, Christian Identity was again brought to the public's attention as Randy Weaver, a follower of Identity and the faith of "Yahweh," fought 200 federal agents from his shack in the high mountains near Naples, Idaho. During the 11-day siege, which left three people dead, including a federal agent, daily news programs explained concepts of the religion to the general public, including the following:

- *Exodus 20:14*: "Thou shalt not commit adultery" is actually an edict from God against intermixing the races.
- *Isaiah 56:3*: "Neither let the son of the stranger, that hath joined himself to the Lord speak, saying, 'The Lord hath utterly separated me from his people.'" Christian Identity translates *strangers* to mean non-whites, indicating that God wants the races to live separately.
- *Luke 4*: "And the devil, taking Jesus up into the high mountain, showed unto him all the kingdoms of the world in a moment of time. And the devil said unto him, 'All this power I will give thee, and the glory of them: for that is delivered unto me and to whomsoever I will give it.'" Identity says that *kingdoms* refer to

today's government authorities and lawmakers. They quote: "And Jesus answered and said unto him, 'Get thee behind me Satan: for it is written, "Thou shalt worship the Lord thy God, and him only shalt thou serve."'" This passage, according to Christian Identity followers, who watched the ordeal from behind police lines during the standoff, is a mandate for Weaver to defy the government and follow God's commandments. His eternity, they said, is incumbent on his obedience to God's law.

"*Yahweh* is an Old Testament term for God," said James Aho, a professor of sociology at Idaho State University. Aho said Yahweh followers believe God encompasses not only love and mercy, but also "terrible violence and unspeakable horrors."

Randy Weaver was not a skinhead, but he was known by neo-Nazi skinheads who had met him at the Aryan Nations compound in Idaho. His 11-day standoff attracted skinheads to the area from Portland, Seattle, and Nevada. In fact, one day during the siege, five skinheads from Portland were arrested as they attempted to transport a large cache of rifles to Weaver's cabin.

It's safe to assume that skinheads from other parts of the country followed the ordeal in the media, lent their support in spirit, and, after it was over, proclaimed Weaver a martyr. Christian Identity considered the incident as free advertising, no doubt attractive to many skinheads who looked upon the event as glamorous.

Racial Hatred Justified

Christian Identity justifies the racial hatred of skinheads and other white supremacists by teaching a rewritten version of Genesis. In the modified form, God created all the races on the third day, except for the whites. These early attempts at creating humans were experiments that failed; in other words, God, that perfect God we learned about as children in Sunday school, screwed up. It wasn't until the last day, the day he made Adam, a white man, that he got it right. Then he formed a woman from Adam's rib and blew life into each of them, thus giving only the white race the status of human. This can be seen, Identity teaches, in the Sanskrit word *human*, which means ho-man or spirit man, the fair-haired white people.

Some Identity followers believe the black race was created early to serve the white man. To support the belief that blacks are not human, some Christian Identity churches circulate literature that establishes a scientific link between the ape and the Negro, such as animal wool, melon-shaped head, small brain, animal smell, long arms, black color, weak lower limbs, outward-turned lips, forward-canted ape pelvis, and large feet.

Yet another Identity version says that Cain's children went off into the woods where they mated with animals to produce the lowly, less-than-human nonwhites.

The result of these beliefs is that they provide a justifi-cation, a sense of goodness and righteousness to the fol-lowers' prejudicial acts. By accepting these teachings as the truth, the followers feel superior to those who do not. Believing they are morally right, the followers have no qualms about their violence toward nonwhites. They act without conscience and with no more concern than they would have stepping on a bug.

> Four skinheads jumped an Amerasian boy as he waited for a bus. They punched him, knocked him to the ground, and executed a boot party, kicking his head and body and stomping his fingers. As they ran off laughing and congratulating each other, one skin looked down and noticed blood on his clothes. "Oh damn," he said irritably, as if he had only dropped some crumbs on his lap. "I went and got gook blood splattered on me."

THE SPREAD OF CHRISTIAN IDENTITY

Christian Identity has been practiced by paramilitary groups on the East Coast, survivalist camps across the Midwest, and the Aryan Nations in Idaho. The religion is followed by a variety of racially conscious people, organizations, groups, and skinhead gangs. Its racist tenets have helped bring together under one umbrella a geographically scattered and oftentimes feuding assortment of white supremacy followers.

Christian Identity also recruits naive and racially unaffected people into the religion. Once in, they come into contact with those in the white supremacist movement. If they accept the teachings and find comfort with those already involved, they become converts.

Since Christian Identity churches are not always out in the open and clearly marked, it's unknown how many there are in the United States. In the late 1980s, the Anti-Defamation League estimated around 50 major Identity preachers in the country, with somewhere between 7,000 and 20,000 followers. With the growth of the skinhead movement, this number is probably larger today.

CHAPTER 8

Pastor Richard Butler's Aryan Nations sits among rugged pine forests near Hayden Lake, Idaho. Since the 1970s, Butler's compound has been visited by the who's who among followers of white supremacy: Tom Metzger, Louis Beam, Robert Mathews, Robert Miles, Carl Franklin, William Pierce, Glenn Miller, and a host of other movers and shakers.

Each April on the weekend closest to the twentieth, Adolph Hitler's birthday, Aryan Nations hosts an Aryan Youth Action Conference for skinheads. This activity-packed, three-day event begins on Friday and ends on Sunday afternoon. The days and evenings are filled with speeches, sporting events, self-defense classes, songs, and church services.

In July, Butler hosts the Aryan World Congress, an event that draws upper-echelon white supremacists and a few skinheads from all over the country. The event is seen as an umbrella under which all the usually splintered Klansmen, neo-Nazis, survivalists, militant tax resisters, and, since 1990, skinheads, can meet, talk about the past year, plan, and share beliefs.

Aryan Nations was formed at a time when the David Duke Klan was looked upon by impatient white supremacists as being too passive. At Aryan Nations, they

ARYAN NATIONS

A gathering of skinheads and other neo-Nazis at Aryan Nations in Idaho.

found an active, violence-prone organization offering them far more than David Duke's vision. They liked the Aryan Nations' advocacy of paramilitary training, and they were especially fond of what Aryan Nations called "Territorial Imperative," a plan that would separate races geographically in the United States.

Aryan Nations' militant approach to white supremacy has spawned such groups as The Order and The Order II. The Order based its violent but short-lived series of crimes on *The Turner Diaries,* a novel by National Alliance leader William Pierce, using the pseudonym Andrew Macdonald. This novel is about a white revolutionary group called The Order that used bombings, murder, counterfeit money, poisoning, and, eventually, nuclear weapons to fight an international race war.

The real Order, led by a zealot named Robert Mathews, emulated much of the fictional Order's adventures. Before they were all captured between late 1984 and 1985, they killed a state trooper, a talkative Aryan Nations' member, and Allen Berg, a Denver talk show host. They passed counterfeit money, robbed two armored cars of more than $4 million, and held up two

*A typical poster displaying
the Aryan Nations' name.*

banks. Their 18-month crime spree prompted the largest FBI operation against domestic violence in the history of the United States. Robert Mathews was subsequently killed in a blazing shoot-out with FBI agents in Washington state.

The FBI and other informed sources believe the stolen money was distributed to an assortment of white supremacy groups around the country, including Richard Butler's Aryan Nations and WAR leader Tom Metzger. It should come as no surprise that these two leaders adamantly deny receiving a penny.

In 1986, Order II picked up where the first Order left off. The first Order had 24 members, but Order II—or as they liked to call themselves, Bruders Schweigen Strike Force II—had only four members. Nonetheless, their short crime spree included the bombing of a federal building and several houses in Coeur d'Alene, Idaho, circulating counterfeit money, killing a man, and plotting robberies. All four revolutionaries were captured and subsequently plead guilty to their crimes.

The Aryan Nations' criminal activities were not restricted to Idaho, however. In 1990, around the time of Tom Metzger's civil trial in Portland, Oregon, three Aryan Nations' members were arrested for plotting to bomb synagogues and a gay bar in Seattle. A year later, an Aryan Nations member was arrested for firing a gun in a Nashville synagogue. In 1992, a skinhead living at Aryan Nations was arrested for the shooting death of another skinhead just outside the compound grounds.

Amazingly, Richard Butler has never been prosecuted for any of the activity that has come out of the Aryan Nations compound. After the roundup of the first Order, Butler was charged with illegally plotting to overthrow the United States government but was acquitted in 1988. Although he has been careful to keep himself removed from the crimes that have been generated at or near his compound, he often gives support to the activists. For example, he referred to members of the Order as "virile young men" and said he could understand the frustration that led to their crimes. He publicly deplored the violence of Order II, claiming he had no connection to the group. He even offered a $1,000 reward for their capture.

WHO IS RICHARD BUTLER?

Richard Butler, a former aerospace engineer, learned about Christian Identity in California as a follower of ex-Klansman Wesley Swift. While attending his church, Butler met an assortment of key players in the white supremacy movement, including William Potter Gale, who was to become a leader in the Posse Comitatus movement.

Butler moved to Idaho in the 1970s, leaving behind in California a police record for weapons violations and a charge of lewd conduct near a schoolyard. He has made vague attempts to explain away the latter charge, but few people know the accurate story.

During the 1970s, Butler carved his compound out of 20 acres in the forests near Hayden Lake. He envisioned a homeland for Aryans only, inviting white families to the area. In a short time, his compound, surrounded by a six-foot-high barbed wire fence and patrolled by Doberman pinschers, became what he had envisioned: a unifying force for the various white supremacist organizations and individual followers.

In the early 1980s, he launched a successful prison ministry, mailing copies of his newsletter, *The Way,* to convicts. To help him recruit, he used members of the Aryan Brotherhood, a white supremacist prison gang still found in most prisons today. Although he used his religion to make contact, he was more interested in drafting soldiers to his militant cause than parishioners. He often extended them refuge at his compound when they had been released from prison.

In 1981, he held his first Aryan World Congress, attended by white supremacists from all around the country. The event has been held every year except 1985, the year The Order was stopped and all was thrown into chaos for Butler. The three-day gathering is similar to the Aryan Youth Conference held in April. There are speeches, workshops, and an exhibition area where attendees can buy and sell literature, tapes, and various goods relating to white supremacy. Many of the speeches are about how Jews are responsible for the large number of missing children and how blacks are less than human. Workshops teach attendees how to get fake IDs, how to conduct terrorist activity, and how to use applicable military techniques.

Butler is not afraid to change with the times. A few years ago, he sensed that skinheads were the new generation of white supremacists. He saw that their youth and their willingness to act out violently were the shot in the arm the movement needed. In 1990, he started the Aryan Youth Congress at his compound for the younger set. Realizing that skinheads have little money and are incapable of moving in large numbers to the Northwest, northern Idaho in particular, he decided to take the movement to them. He frequently appoints visiting skinheads as his representatives to go back to their towns and pass on his teachings. Periodically, he sends out representatives from the compound who have the knowledge and ability to speak for him.

As a pastor of the Christian Identity Church of Jesus Christ Christian located inside his Aryan Nations compound, Butler conducts sermons that, by all reports, would cure an insomniac. He is also called on by young skinhead lovers to officiate at their weddings; these ceremonies take place in the compound chapel, under a large flag bearing a swastika. Children of the congregation attend classes where they must recite the pledge of allegiance with this twist, "We are one Aryan nation under God."

As of this writing, Butler is in declining health. Skinheads returning from events at the compound report they see less and less of Butler each visit. The question bandied about by law enforcement officials is, who will take his place? Will it be someone who will continue Butler's legacy, or will it be someone with a fresh burst of energy who will work to build a hotter fire under the movement? Will it be someone who will advocate more violence?

Klanwatch Director Danny Welch predicts that Aryan Nations will continue after Butler steps down and perhaps be stronger than ever. He believes the new attention that Aryan Nations is focusing on skinheads and the reverence skins have for Richard Butler, combined with the hateful rhetoric Aryan Nations and Christian Identity are noted for, all add up to a deadly mix that will spark future problems.

"Aryan Nations has been and will continue to be a dangerous group because of its notorious reputation for violence and its wide-ranging influence among white supremacists across the country," Welch contends.

CHAPTER 9

Ss there a tie between skinheads and the Ku Klux Klan? As with many issues concerning skinheads, the answer is not crystal clear. We can say that not all skinheads associate with the Klan, but enough of them do for it to be of concern to law enforcement. And those who do associate with the Klan do so at varying levels of involvement—some deep, some not so deep. While there are some obvious indicators that show a connection, it is easy to make false assumptions.

Kids like expressions. Parents and teachers of teenagers know how hard it is to keep up with their language. One expression that is commonplace in many schools, high schools in particular, is "KKK." "He's KKK," a kid will say about another student. Or, "That girl hates minorities. She's definitely KKK."

Racial tension and racial issues are commonplace in many schools today. As a result, in some areas of the country, kids use the expression "KKK" when referring to someone who has verbally or physically expressed hatred of or anger toward a minority person. It may be that the person the kids are referring to is a white supremacist; but do not automatically assume this means the Ku Klux Klan is in the school. More than likely, the kids are using the term generically.

SKINHEADS AND THE KU KLUX KLAN

THE REAL KLAN

The 1980s was an erratic period for the Ku Klux Klan, consisting of short-lived highs and devastating lows. But through it all the Klan survived.

In the early 1980s, the Ku Klux Klan enjoyed a burst of popularity in part from its changing image created by David Duke, then leader of the Knights of the Ku Klux Klan. He wore a business suit instead of a white sheet and was the darling of talk shows and a frequent guest on college campuses. He presented an image of a clean-cut, handsome Robert Redford, articulate and reasonable in his politics. He was so smooth and persuasive that he could sell iceboxes at the North Pole.

Several long-time white supremacists took advantage of the improved image and ran for public office. Although none of them won, some came close. Harold Covington, Nazi leader in South Carolina, picked up 56,006 votes in the primary for attorney general, 42.8 percent of the ballot. Tom Metzger won the Democratic congressional primary in California, subsequently losing in the general election. In Detroit, Gerald R. Carlson, a Nazi, won 55 percent of the vote for the Republican nomination for Congress.

By the mid-1980s, the newness had worn off. The media attention the Klan had been enjoying was diminishing and they were losing members. More radical white supremacists were moving into the limelight, such as tax protesters, paramilitary groups, Posse Comitatus, Aryan Nations, and Order I and Order II.

Aggressive law enforcement, however, quickly put most of these groups behind bars. Additionally, three major Klan groups in the south were destroyed by criminal and civil convictions against their members.

The prisons became a breeding ground for organized racism. Then the movement got a positive shot in the arm when several white supremacists who had been involved directly or indirectly with The Order's crime spree were acquitted of sedition charges.

In the mid to late 1980s, just at the point when the Ku Klux Klan and other white supremacy organizations were at their weakest, racist skinheads emerged onto the scene. They were immediately seen by these groups as the strong arm to get things rolling again. The late Robert Miles, a Christian Identity preacher in Michigan and former Grand Dragon of the Realm of Michigan in the United Klans of America, remarked in 1988:

> "If there is a future for the right wing, skinheads will be the first racial wave. They're what Nazi storm troopers were in the early '20s."

Tom Metzger, who had been the former Grand Dragon of the Ku Klux Klan in California, called skinheads "front-line warriors." Metzger, along with Richard Butler and other white supremacist leaders, began immediately to actively vie for attention from racist skinheads. As the growing presence of skinheads and their crimes were played up in the media, the Klan and other racist groups once again began getting attention.

Over the past few turbulent years, as the popularity of the Klan rose, fell, and rose again, their basic beliefs never changed: they still fear and hate minorities and look forward to the race war. One Klan leader put it this way:

> "There will be an economic collapse, riots in the cities, famine, and war. People will kill each other for food, weapons, shelter, clothing, anything. It will get so bad that parents will eat their children, blacks will rape and kill white women, and homosexuals will sodomize whoever they can. It is time now that people woke up to the conspiracy in America and prepared themselves with weapons, food, and supplies, in a rural area away from the cities."

SKINHEADS AND THE KLAN TODAY

Today, hardly a month passes without the Klan, skinheads, and other racist groups showing up on talk shows.

A flier showing the link between the KKK and racist skinheads.

Producers know that the audience loves to hate these guests. It's almost routine now for Geraldo Rivera to get assaulted by a skinhead or neo-Nazi on his program. When the dust clears and Geraldo has been bandaged, two things have happened: the show got good ratings, and the white supremacy movement got new followers.

The exposure of skinheads and their overt activities helps the Klan by giving racism lots of attention. The Klan in turn educates the skinheads through its literature and activities. Today it's common to see the Ku Klux Klan and skinheads side by side as they march or rally against or in honor of something.

In Birmingham, Alabama, 45 skinheads and Klansmen marched through the downtown streets to rally at a Confederate memorial in a city park. The Klan was represented by the Aryan White Knights from Georgia and the White Knights of the Ku Klux Klan from Florida. Skinheads were represented by members of the Confederate Hammer Skins and the Aryan National Front. Three hundred officers in riot gear kept the peace during the event.

•

In Aurora, Colorado, 60 Klansmen and skinheads held a rally that drew 450 protesters and required 300 police to keep the peace.

•

In London, Kentucky, 50 Ku Klux Klan members and several neo-Nazi skinheads marched through the streets after hearing an anti-Jewish speech by a Klan leader. They later gathered at a farm and burned a cross as 200 protesters shouted in anger.

•

In Watkinsville, Georgia, Klansmen, neo-Nazis, skinheads, and survivalists marched through town and distributed literature.

•

In Portland, Oregon, a neo-Nazi skinhead gang called Southern Justice became affiliated with the Confederated Knights of the Ku Klux Klan in Clarkton, Missouri.

Skinhead artwork depicting the American flag with several symbols of hate.

In Denver, Colorado, around 125 Klansmen and skinheads gathered on Martin Luther King's birthday to rally at the same time 12,000 people honoring Martin Luther King were scheduled to march by. Before the event was over, 21 people had been arrested, police officers had received injuries, buses had their windows broken out, several police cars had been damaged, and one police car had been overturned and vandalized.

As we roll along through the 1990s, skinheads and the Ku Klux Klan will continue to work together for their cause. They will rally and march together, adding strength

KLAN TERMINOLOGY

EMPIRE	The national Ku Klux Klan organization
REALM	The Klan in a particular state
DOMINION	Five or more counties of a realm
PROVINCE	One to three counties in dominion
KLANTON or DEN	Local chapter
KLAVERN	Local meeting place
IMPERIAL WIZARD	Head of national Ku Klux Klan
GRAND DRAGON	Head of a realm
GREAT TITAN	Head of a dominion
GIANT	Head of a province
EXALTED CYCLOPS	Head of a klanton
KLALIFF	Vice president to Exalted Cyclops
KLADD	Assistant Exalted Cyclops
KLEAGLE	An organizer
KLUDD	Chaplain
KLOKARD	National lecturer

and numbers to their efforts. Skinheads will continue to be demonstrative in their expression of white supremacy, while the Klan will benefit from the skins' actions without having to go to jail. The Klan will continue to be the educators of the young warriors through its literature and activities. It's even common now for skinheads to distribute fliers with post office boxes belonging to the Klan.

And an educated assumption is that we will see skinheads who have grown too old for their boots and shaved heads graduate to the uniform of the Ku Klux Klan.

CHAPTER 10

White supremacists argue that it's called *cross lighting* while everyone else refers to it as *cross burning*. Semantically, it's six of one and a half-dozen of the other, but the real significance lies in the symbolism it evokes in the minds of the people who celebrate it and in the minds of its intended victims.

A LITTLE HISTORY

The burning cross can be traced back to the Celtic, Nordic, and Teutonic peoples of twelfth-century Europe. During those times, the tribes kept large stacks of wood or large, wooden crosses on the highest point of land near where they lived. When lookouts detected invaders, the wood or crosses were set ablaze to alert everyone for miles around of the approaching danger. An adjacent tribe would see the warning signal burning on top of the hill or cliff and light their wood to warn their people, as well as the next tribe. The tribe members, called clansmen, would gather at the fires and decide how they were going to deal with the invasion.

THE KU KLUX KLAN

Centuries later, the Ku Klux Klan adopted cross burning/lighting as part of its ceremony, one Klansmen

CROSS BURNING

Sometimes a swastika is lit so that its symbolism can shine into the night.

claim is religious in its significance. When asked why they burn the symbol of Christianity if the act is supposed to be religious, they adamantly deny they are burning and destroying the cross, but are rather lighting it, illuminating it so all the world can see their Christian way.

This explanation is true on the surface. They are showing off their Christian beliefs, but their beliefs are based on racism and hatred. The burning cross has been used for years as both a unifying symbol among white supremacists and as a weapon of intimidation against people of color, most often blacks.

CROSS BURNING TODAY

The ritual of igniting a large cross when white supremacists have gathered brings together all the racist factions. As the participants encircle the fire, chanting white supremacist rhetoric, snapping out stiff-armed Nazi salutes, and basking in the glory of being white, people cloaked in white sheets, Nazi uniforms, and skinhead regalia are unified, at least momentarily, in the reflection of the flames.

Today, setting a cross ablaze in the yard of a black family is a blatant symbol of an earlier time when the old Ku Klux Klan wantonly terrorized blacks in the South. Although we now live in post-civil-rights times and many states have laws against the act, cross burning is still used as a device to frighten people.

> A 17-year-old skinhead in Dubuque, Iowa, was sentenced to 10 years in prison for setting a cross on fire at the home of a black family. In a plea bargain, the skinhead pleaded guilty to second-degree arson.

It's common for skinheads to burn a cross when they gather to party on a farm or on a river bank. The scene can be chilling to an uninvolved observer as a dozen or more skinheads with shaved heads, flight jackets, and Doc Marten boots drunkenly sway in the glow of a burning cross and chant, "Sieg Heil! Sieg Heil! Sieg Heil!" as they repeatedly snap out the Nazi salute.

Skinheads also burn crosses for the purpose of intimidating blacks of mixed-race couples. Although skinheads are seldom caught in the act, graffiti—such as "White Power," "Skins Rule," and swastika symbols—found at or near the crime scene indicate that a skinhead gang was most likely involved.

OTHER PEOPLE BURN CROSSES TOO

On the other hand, not all cross burnings are perpetrated by skinheads. The burning may be the result of an ongoing feud between neighbors, usually a black family and a white family. The conflict may be over a noisy stereo or kids running across the neighbors' yard, issues that have nothing to do with racism. The white neighbor, however, uses a cross burning and its symbolism as a sure way to strike back at the black family.

PUBLICITY HELPS POLICE

As mentioned, few suspects are apprehended for cross burnings, simply because the incidents occur during the hours of darkness and the perpetrators flee undetected into the night. However, when the burning is done by skinheads and the incident receives media attention—and they do love to give it top billing—there is a greater chance you will find out who was responsible.

If you stop a couple of skinheads on the street to engage them in friendly conversation or you arrest them for an unrelated incident, ask them what they know about the burning. It's highly doubtful they will admit their involvement, but they may inform on someone else who was there, especially if the person is an enemy or in a rival gang.

STATISTICS AND VICTIMS

Organizations that monitor hate activity across the country list several reported cross burnings every month. These statistics, however, reflect only reported incidents, so their numbers are actually fewer than those actually committed. It's safe to say that many cross burning go unreported because the victims are afraid to tell the police. They do not want the attention, or they are afraid of a reprisal or copycat burning. Also affecting the statistics' accuracy is the fact that not all police agencies report their incidents of cross burnings to the monitoring organizations.

Victims of cross burnings need to be treated with sensitivity and compassion. Although in your jurisdiction the crime may only be a trespass or a burning violation, the symbolism of the act can be traumatic to the victims. They will be angry, fearful, confused, and possibly suspicious of you.

CHAPTER 11

As skinheads continue to expand in number and activities, they will continue to affiliate with other organizations to further their educations, to participate in activities, and to derive a sense of significance from rubbing shoulders with big names in the movement.

We have already discussed the association of skinheads with the KKK and Christian Identity. Below are brief descriptions of several other organizations that, at least in part, share the same beliefs as neo-Nazi skinheads.

This list is certainly not complete since the white supremacy movement is constantly changing to meet the needs of the times. Organizations only marginally involved with skinheads today may be in close association with them tomorrow, and new groups, whose influence we cannot now gauge, may already be forming.

POSSE COMITATUS

Posse followers base much of their ideology on their interpretation of the congressional Posse Comitatus Act that was passed after the Civil War. The act specifically banned the federal military from intervening in local police matters. It came about because President Grant had been using troops to guard ballot boxes to prevent voting fraud. Congress, how-

VARIOUS AFFILIATIONS

Third Position posters often defend white workers.

ever, proclaimed that such police powers could only come from the county level since federal troops were prohibited from enforcing domestic laws.

Posse Comitatus followers today have taken the doctrine a step beyond to mean that no citizen has to obey any authority higher than the county sheriff. The Posse believes they do not have to pay income taxes, make Social Security payments, buy license plates, or even get a driver's license. Some Posse followers even believe that the doctrine was delivered to man by God and that to pay taxes is illegal and sinful. Posse beliefs are infused with Christian Identity theology, the same theology skinheads follow.

Posse Comitatus has had a violent history over the past 20 years. The followers are usually heavily armed, and they are known to conduct paramilitary exercises and survivalist training. They have had numerous deadly confrontations with law enforcement.

At this time, it's unknown how much involvement exists between skinheads and the Posse Comitatus. What is known is that the two groups share many of the same beliefs and goals. If skinheads have not yet associated with the Posse, it's only a matter of time until they do.

POPULISTS

Populists are conservatives with anti-Semitic beliefs. As with Christian Identity followers, they believe the Jews run the government, the media, and the banks. They frequently support Posse Comitatus and Christian Identity followers to run for public office, though they rarely win. Skinheads are often used to hand out voting literature in support of the candidates.

David Duke was a Populist who lost his bid for president but managed to win a seat in the Louisiana State House as a Democrat.

RACIAL SURVIVALISTS

Racial survivalists are fanatics, many of them Christian Identity followers, who believe in the pending race war. They live in communes and practice military tactics and survival training. In the past, they stockpiled illegal weapons and explosives, including land mines.

Intelligence information comes in continually about skinheads in remote areas practicing war games, shooting assault weapons, and living off the land in the style of the survivalist.

THIRD POSITION

The Third Position, sometimes called Aryan Socialism, is more of a concept than an organization. Its followers claim to be neither liberal nor conservative, but say they are the protectors of the white working class.

Many believe that the Third Position is the creation of WAR leader Tom Metzger, who believes that political parties are a joke and that the federal government is ruled by Jews and white race traitors, thus making government an enemy of all white people.

Joe Grego, head of the Oklahoma White Man's Association, believes in the Third Position. He tells whites to arm themselves and get ready for the impending revolution. He encourages his followers with this rhetoric:

> "The Aryan army is preparing to take over the land which is rightfully ours. The guns are loaded; the people are ready."

Skinhead literature, much of it obtained through Metzger's WAR paper, supports the Third Position philosophy.

SEPARATISTS

Separatists, sometimes called Nationalists, want a separate nation for whites and minorities. Many Klansmen, neo-Nazis, and racist skinheads support this idea. As is often the case, the various white supremacist groups cannot agree on how this should be accomplished. One leader states simply that all nonwhites should be deported. Another believes that whites should claim the southern states, while another leader wants the Northwest: Oregon, Washington, Idaho, Montana, and Wyoming, and a little of Canada.

Often Separatists claim to not be racist. They say all they want is for people to be separated by color and race, which, they argue, would make them get along better. Most separatists, racist skinheads for sure, are really racists who are trying to appear less threatening. Some upper-echelon leaders use the Separatist ideology as a way of hooking the naive into their folds. Once they're inside, the facade drops, thus revealing the group's real cause.

Racist skinheads commonly tell police that they are not racists but simply Separatists. They will say something to the effect that they are proud to be white just as blacks are proud to be black, and everything would be better if the races could just live separately.

CHURCH OF THE CREATOR

Ben Klassen holds the self-appointed rank of Pontifex Maximus in the religion he created and calls Church of the Creator. The church is an internationally known white supremacist organization based in the Appalachian Mountains town of Otto, North Carolina. Under the heading of religion, Klassen has put together a plan for worldwide white revolution, a plan that uses any force necessary, to include, as he puts it, "murder, treachery, lying, deceit, mass killing, whatever it takes."

Klassen works to recruit prisoners and skinheads into his organization, which is now located in more than 20 states and eight foreign countries. His dogma is basic racism: "Our race is our religion. What is good for the white race is of the highest virtue, and what is bad for the white race is the ultimate sin." The Church of the Creator's creed declares null and void any law deemed contrary to the goal of white supremacy. Its slogan is "RaHoWa": Racial Holy War.

This so-called religion has nothing to do with theology. There is no deity, no worship service, and no scripture, other than Klassen's writings. He has written eight books and produced 68 newspapers, all of which encourage violence, if necessary, to reach worldwide domination.

In 1989, Klassen set up the "School for Gifted Boys." He said, "We will take young men and prepare them to break Jews like matchsticks, not just physically, but intellectually."

The strict, no-nonsense dogma is appealing to some skinheads. Those who have served time in prison are promoted to the rank of "reverend" by Klassen. Even skinheads currently behind bars are still able to remain active in the church, since Klassen uses freedom of religion to get his reading material inside the walls. Some prisoners have even demanded the right to hold services to discuss their racist religion.

CHAPTER 12

For years, skinheads and other white supremacists have been talking about a race war. For a long time, they claimed it was going to happen in 1995. In 1991, skinheads moved the date forward to the summer of 1992—one skinhead even got specific and pinpointed the first shot to occur somewhere near Chicago. Well, it didn't happen, but the Los Angeles riots occurred in the spring of 1992, and many skinheads thought (hoped) that was the beginning of it.

We can sit and laugh at the stupidity of such a concept, but we must keep in mind that many of these people believe deeply that a race war is going to take place. We know some white supremacists are stockpiling weapons in preparation for the anticipated battle. A year before the race war was to begin in 1992, many police agencies were receiving information about large caches of assault weapons hidden by skinhead gangs. Though the war failed to materialize, some of the weapons have surfaced. *Some* is the significant word here.

Richard Butler of Aryan Nations preaches that the great battle will take place in America's Grain Belt. "Those fields would make an ideal place for a tank battle between the United States and the Soviet Union. And it will be a great battle between two white armies."

THE RACE WAR

This flier perpetuates the fantasy of a race war.

This common belief among all the white supremacist organizations is one of the threads that ties them together. From New York to Nebraska to Illinois to Colorado to Washington to Texas, they await Armageddon, their weapons stockpiled and their delusions of grandeur bubbling with anticipation.

The following text is from a skinhead flier distributed at a rally (the punctuation and capitalization are entirely theirs):

SO YOU WANT A RACE WAR, EH?

The majority of the people in the White Power movement believes, and quite justly so, that in our near future there looms an event relevant to all as the Race War. Most people cannot help but see this prophecy as fact, when confronted with the hordes of non-White dredge in our vast cities . . . with the conditions the way they are in these times, it is a wonder such a drastic event has not become a reality already! For a number of you who preach such a belief and feel ready for such an incredible conflict, get ready for a not so wonderful surprise . . . YOU ARE DEAD MEAT! Sit down and think for a moment just what we are up against. Tanks, jets, HUNDREDS OF THOUSANDS of well armed men, question; right now, this second, are you prepared to fight a guerrilla war? Do not make excuses for yourself, there are only two choices you can make, yes and no, just as there are only two ways you can exist on this earth, dead or alive, free man or slave. There is no middle ground! The Vietcong during the Vietnam war lived their lives in a constant state of preparedness for war, and you know who won that conflict! Let us learn from their example. Any person who speaks of any kind of war must be prepared for it! Do not slack off and expect your racial peers to risk their survival and time to baby you along and teach you how to survive when the final conflict comes upon us. A time will come when you will not be able to sleep in your nice heated little home, in a comfy bed. Most likely you will be living ten miles from nowhere in the woods, in a shelter made out of scavenged materials. THAT is what survivalists are all about, so you had better GET USED TO IT! The key to a White victory is KNOWLEDGE. Take the necessary time NOW to learn wilderness survival, field medicine, combat crafts, and so on. BE WARNED, when the day comes, you will have to do your part, act seriously, and take steps to be prepared. The choice is yours, you can talk big for now, but when the day comes, if you cannot pull your weight, you will be on your own. For your sake and the White race, do not let this happen!

USING THE POLICE

White supremacists cannot agree on how police officers are to be used during the race war. Some white supremacists want to use them, while others argue that they cannot be trusted.

Those in favor of recruiting police officers contend that the police already have the skills the movement so desperately needs.

> The cops are the Jews' first line of defense, but they can just as easily come over to our side, wholesale, and be our first line of defense. If we show them that we represent their interests, we can use the cops as a tool in our arsenal and make the taxpayer pick up the tab.

Others, however, believe in the white supremacist's golden rule of never trusting the police, FBI, or any agents of ZOG.

CHAPTER 13

Other than arresting skinheads and other gang members for committing crimes and patrolling their rallies to keep them peaceful, one of the most effective ways police officers can do battle against these groups is by educating citizens as to their existence and their dangers. There are several ways of doing this.

PRESENTATIONS

You either like to do these or you hate them. Getting up in front of audiences and giving presentations on gangs goes with the territory. When gangs come to town and citizens and young gang members begin to get hurt, the public wants to know what is going on. To find out, they call the experts—the police. Although presentations can be as much of a pain as media interviews, both can be just as beneficial to the police as they are to the public. As a result of Portland officers giving hundreds of presentations to myriad audiences in the community, citizens are now more informed about gangs and thus better able to give the police good information. What they have learned from us has empowered them to take measures to protect themselves and to work in their own neighborhoods to eradicate gang houses.

We also give presentations to

WORKING WITH THE COMMUNITY

law enforcement agencies who are just beginning to see gangs in their jurisdictions. We tell them what policing methods have worked well for us and how to avoid the same mistakes we have made.

We meet weekly with parole and probation officers and discuss who has been doing what to whom during the week. Once a month, the media and social service people meet to hear our presentation on gang activity and the trends we are seeing.

We have developed several outlines for a variety of different audiences and durations. We have outlines for community meetings, college classes, business people, and law enforcement and church groups, ranging in length from 20 minutes to four hours. The problem of gangs in the community is not just a police concern. Since the infestation affects neighborhoods, schools, and businesses, it's everyone's concern. Educating others pays off. It's important that people know how to recognize a gang and have an understanding of its dynamics. An informed public is quicker than an uninformed one to recognize gang activity, report it to the police, and then work in a partnership to eradicate the problem.

WORKING WITH NEIGHBORHOOD ORGANIZATIONS

Working in a partnership with the community has proven beneficial in ridding neighborhoods of gangs. Let's say there is a skinhead house where continual rowdiness has all the neighbors fearful. The first step that you must take is to inform the people living in the neighborhood that the situation is not just a police problem, but a community problem as well, and as such requires the efforts of both to correct.

This starts with a neighborhood meeting, either in a volunteer's home or a community center. Fliers about the meeting should be distributed to all the houses in the neighborhood, or you can use a phone tree to make contact. It's important that everyone knows about it (everyone except the skinheads), so that as many people as possible can participate.

The neighborhood beat car and the police intelligence officer working skinheads should attend. A superior officer is always nice for public relations purposes, showing the public that the police hierarchy is serious about combating the problem. He or she also has the authority to offer specific police services.

The meeting should begin with the intelligence officer and the beat officer providing an overview of skinheads in general and any specifics they know about the skinhead house in question. Unless the officers know all the people in attendance, they should use caution in saying anything that could cause problems if the meeting has been infiltrated by someone from the skinhead house. It's a common practice for skinheads to attend community meetings—remember they don't all have bald heads and always wear boots.

The neighbors are going to have lots of questions and information for the police. For every five naive questions they have, there will be some neighbors who have good information, things they have seen at the skinhead house. For a variety of reasons, some people will not call the police when they see something going on. When officers are in the same room, however, they are more willing to talk.

With everyone present, collective minds can decide what measures to take to solve the problem. The police can provide information on what the department can do, while the neighbors can volunteer to watch the skinhead house, get license plate numbers, get descriptions of people, set up a citizen patrol, take photographs from their windows, talk to the skinhead's landlord, etc.

THINGS A NEIGHBORHOOD CAN DO

People are going to ask you what they can do to help. Below are nine suggestions that not only help the police but get the neighborhood involved in combating the gang problem.

1. *Report all crimes and gang activity*. Call 911 at the first sign of activity. If residents wait too long, the problem may entrench itself and become even more difficult to eradicate. The police rely on neighbors' reports.

2. *Organize a block watch*. Neighbors should organize to enhance their strength and share information. Gangs know there is strength in numbers; neighbors can use the same principle.

3. *Be visible*. Neighborhoods where people work and play in their yards, walk their dogs, pick up litter, and simply show a visible presence are less likely to have criminal gangs moving about.

4. *Take pictures*. Neighbors can take photos and video footage of any activity. Be sure to warn them not to risk their safety for the pictures.

5. *Remove graffiti*. Painting over graffiti works more times than not. It sends out a message that the neighborhood belongs to people who care about it and who are not going to stand still for gang activity.

6. *Get involved with young people*. People should volunteer their time to schools, churches, parks, and neighborhood community centers. This provides positive alternatives to kids other than hanging out and running in packs. It's time to teach kids a positive value system and let kids know that people want to be involved with them.

7. *Be aware and stay informed*. People who are ignorant of the issue and have their heads in the clouds will not see the early warnings of gangs in their neighborhood. Knowledge is power.

8. *Develop an attitude of zero tolerance* . People should stamp out racism, sexism, homophobia, anti-Semitism, and all other forms of bigotry in their community.

9. *Educate neighbors*. People should work within their community to help educate their neighbors about hate crimes and work together to make their neighborhood a safe place for all people.

WHAT ARE HATE CRIMES?

- Hate crimes are motivated by prejudice based on a person's perceived race, color, religion, national origin, sexual orientation, or political beliefs.
- They can take the form of graffiti, vandalism, telephone harassment, assault, intimidation, offensive physical contact, and murder. The motivation is based on the victim's perceived race, color, religion, national origin, or sexual orientation.
- It's a felony when two or more people intimidate or injure a person or damage property, or threaten him in a way that causes him to fear harm to himself or his property.

WHAT VICTIMS SHOULD DO

- Get medical attention.
- Take photos of injuries as soon as possible.
- Take photos of property damage.
- Keep copies of any written hate harassment.
- Write down the date and time of harassing phone calls.
- If the calls come in on an answering machine, keep the tape for the police.
- Talk to people about their feelings. Know that anger, fear, confusion, depression, and a sense of being alone are all common emotions. Talking about their experience can be an important part of recovery.
- Call the police. Since hate crimes are not always obvious to people who do not know the victim, tell the officer why the incident is a hate crime.
- If not the police, report the incident to a victim advocacy organization. But police will not investigate the incident unless it is reported to them.

THE MEDIA

Most police officers hate the media. This is because the majority of people in police work are conservative, while it seems most people in the media are liberal. Water and oil. The police are deep in the crud, the first to see the victims: the emotionally frantic, scared, mutilated, bloody, and dead. The police are the ones who have to go after the emotional abusers, the mutilators, the killers. Sometimes the bad guys go with the police easily, sometimes they don't.

Most of the time, reporters are not there when the police see the victims or capture the bad guys. But the reporters still have to tell the story. Reporting the news is telling what happened, but it also involves holding on to the viewers' or readers' attention. In short, the story has to inform, but it also has to entertain. In the process of finding this balance, the truth frequently gets distorted.

There is also the issue of cop bashing. The press loves to kick the police when they screw up, keeping the story alive for days, sometimes weeks, or even years. But when the press screws up a story or when police officers are found to be innocent of some accusation previously reported, there is rarely a retraction, or it gets buried on the back pages.

It's easy to see why there is a mistrust of the media. But no matter how much the police complain, the reality is that the media are here to stay. Therefore, it's best to try to establish a workable relationship. Sometimes the effort pays off, sometimes it does not. Some officers complain that they have tried everything to get along with their local press, but there is still no cooperation. Sometimes that is just the way it's going to be.

The Portland Police Bureau has had a good relationship with the press for years. We have a public information officer (PIO) who is the frontline liaison with the press. He is the one the media talk to at crime scenes, and he acts as the primary spokesman for most other news stories that occur within the bureau.

When gangs first reared their ugly heads in Portland, the PIO interfaced with the press, continuing to do so until the problem became so large and complex that the PIO couldn't possibly answer all the questions the press wanted answered about the inner workings of gangs.

In early 1988, the intelligence officers assigned to each of the gangs were told to work with the media. No one was in a better position to know and understand the history and internal workings of gangs, as well as what information could and could not be revealed. We could tell a reporter what happened, as well as explain a gang's politics and philosophy. The result of this openness was that the press got timely, accurate information and was able to present a clear picture of gangs in its stories.

The general public and the police also benefited from this approach. When all the different gangs began in Portland—they all started within one year—the public's naive period was short-lived, primarily because of the excellent working relationship between the police and the media. Through almost nightly news reports, the public quickly became educated as to what gangs looked like and what they were all about.

We found that an informed public was better able to decipher what it was seeing on the street and in its neighborhoods. This helped us because people were, and still are, giving us good information. In fact, since newspaper articles and radio stories quote the officers by name, and television news always displays the officers' names under their faces, people call and ask for them specifically. The press benefits because it always has someone to go to, someone who can speak in detail and provide more information than what is contained in the usual press release.

The issue of trust is a major one, probably more so from the standpoint of the police. Admittedly, one thing that has been helpful in Portland is that the television stations, the major newspapers, and a couple of the larger radio stations all have one or more reporters who consistently work gang stories. They need us. They want to be able to come to our office at any time for information. They cannot afford to blatantly misquote us or to sensationalize an incident to where it affects a police investigation.

Of the hundreds of interviews I have given, I can recall only two stories where reporters twisted the information far beyond the truth. One of the stories went across the country on the wire, and the other, printed in a left-wing rag, deliberately twisted information to maliciously slander me. Needless to say, when these same reporters attempted another interview a few weeks later, they were told they would no longer be given information by the police. We have developed such a good relationship with some of the regular reporters that they often call us with information. Sometimes they hear things before we do, a result of people calling them for publicity.

> I got paged one evening while I was at home by a reporter I had worked with many times. He told me he had just received a call from the leader of the SHARPs about a planned demonstration the next day in front of an apartment building where a neo-Nazi skin lived.
>
> Based on that information, we responded with officers and surprised the SHARPs. So instead of the event catching us off guard and making us look inept, we were able to react proactively and quell a potentially violent situation. In return, I gave the reporter an interview at the scene.

Of course, no matter how good the reporter-police relationship is, stories may still get changed in the newsroom. The officer and the conscientious reporter may agree on how a quote is to be used or even how an entire story should be presented, but it's still possible that an editor may change it before the story goes out. With deadlines and other pressures on an editor, he or she may have more interest in a dramatic headline or a slight twist in the facts than in the relationship the street reporter has so carefully cultivated with the police.

The media are here to stay, and so are the police. Police agencies around the country have discovered that, more times than not, it's more beneficial to work with the press than against it.

Racist Skinheads in the Media

Racist skinheads are often on such talk shows as Sally Jesse Raphael, Oprah Winfrey, Phil Donahue, etc. As much as these hosts like to shake their heads in disgust and affect an "oh, this is so terrible" expression, they nonetheless continue having skinheads and KKK on their programs because they know their audiences will watch.

Tom Metzger and other prominent players in the white supremacy movement have said many times that TV exposure of any kind brings in money for their organizations.

> During Metzger's two-week civil suit trial in Portland, there were never fewer than a dozen media representatives in the court room. *USA Today, People, Newsweek*, and a host of others, including authors with book contracts, jockeyed each day for position to watch the trial and pass notes to Metzger asking for interviews.
>
> At the end of the day, he and his son would shuffle through the notes and decide which magazine, newspaper, or television station would give them the largest audience.

In the late 1980s, skinheads were guests on talk shows even more than they are today. Invitations to the shows began to wane after Geraldo Rivera had his nose broken on his show during a melee involving skinheads, guests, Geraldo, and the show's crew. Since then, many TV programs tighten their security measures when skinheads are on a show, and even then it's common to see visibly frightened hosts.

Some people postulate that media exposure of white supremacists in the late 1980s is what brought about their rapid growth. Maybe. But it's possible that their rapid growth by other means got them the media exposure.

In Portland, there does not seem to be any correlation between media coverage and increased skinhead activity. After the homicide of the Ethiopian man, there was a dramatic and unprecedented increase in activity, but that was a result of several other elements coming together at

A skinhead is interviewed by a television reporter.

the same time. It's important to note that there were racially motivated murders perpetrated by skinheads in two other states that same year, and although those incidents received press coverage, those cities did not experience an increase in activity.

Racist skinheads feel they are being misrepresented in the media. They complain that news stories paint a distorted picture of what they are about. For example, they say it's never reported that they do not use hard drugs (at least the hard-core skinheads). They also complain they are never given credit for holding down jobs rather than "sucking off the welfare system as minorities do."

Antiracist Skinheads in the Media

Antiracist skinheads try to convince the media that they are a group of fine, young, goal-oriented people whose sole purpose is to protect the innocent from the hordes of Nazi scum. The media like this because it's a new twist on the skinhead story. Then, when the antiracist skins commit a crime, usually an assault against a racist skinhead, the media present the story as a big surprise (to everyone except the police). The story is then played up because it presents another angle to the skinhead phenomenon.

This makes the antiracist skins angry because the story contradicts and tarnishes the image they had been trying to perpetuate and puts them in a bad light with certain liberal groups with whom they had hoped to align.

The antiracist skins then try to get back on the good side of the media by doing something press-worthy. They might picket in front of an apartment where a racist skinhead lives or at a business where one works. The ensuing media coverage paints them as knights in shining armor, especially to those viewers who missed the earlier story about their committing a crime. But in time, they will get into trouble again.

CHAPTER 14

It's important to take a brief look at the neo-Nazi skinhead situation in Europe, because what is happening there affects what is going on in the United States.

Many American racist skinheads have a fascination with things German: pins, medals, jackets, World War II uniforms, flags, and posters. We know it's common for some American skinheads to travel to Europe to see what is going on and to make contacts. A trip to Europe is like a shot of adrenaline, the effects of which last for months, maybe even years. One American skinhead who had inherited several thousand dollars treated members of his gang to airline tickets and a concert featuring a white power band in a German city.

After a skinhead-perpetrated murder occurred on the West Coast, news crews from New York and Germany flew in to cover the story and, in particular, to interview racist skinheads. To the New York crew's aggravation, the skinheads would talk only to the Germans because they liked their accent.

Not only are our skinheads watching the hate violence in Europe, but other American hate groups are paying attention too.

SKINHEADS IN EUROPE

Dennis Mahon, ambassador-at-large for the White Knights of the Ku Klux Klan, traveled to Germany and conducted a cross burning in a forest outside Berlin, an event attended by German neo-Nazi skinheads. "The skinheads are doing a hell of a job here," Mahon said. "Every means are justified, I mean use every means to rescue your nation."

German skinheads have carried American Ku Klux Klan literature on their marches and rallies, and it has been found in their possession during their arrests.

The Invisible Empire, Knights of the Ku Klux Klan has worked with Australian Klan members, who report to the North Carolina organization that they're recruiting heavily to give strength to their fight to abolish the rights of Aborigines.

There are frequent news stories coming out of Europe, sometimes nightly, concerning the rising tide of neo-Nazi violence in their cities' streets. It's imperative we keep a watchful eye on developments in Europe because American racist gangs and organizations are watching it carefully.

SINCE THE WALL CAME DOWN

Many observers of the situation in Europe—Germany in particular—compare today's climate to the one that existed there in the 1930s when Adolf Hitler rose to power. The economy in the states of eastern Germany has been falling rapidly since the reunification. More than 40 percent of Germans in the eastern sector are unemployed, and the number is steadily rising. Adding to the problem is the county's liberal immigration policy that permits 120,000 Third World refugees and asylum-seekers to come to Germany every year. Some observers claim an even higher number, somewhere in the range of a thousand a day. Most come from troubled Eastern European countries, including the former Soviet Union, Yugoslavia, Romania, and Bulgaria.

Germany's immigration policy is what angers the young neo-Nazi skinheads. Skinheads chant: "Yesterday the Jews, tomorrow the Turks." Since the fall of the Berlin wall, all the ecstatic cheering and hugging has been replaced by gloom, anger, and racial hatred. The skinheads want to force the foreigners out of Germany through whatever means necessary. Although the East and West German governments invited the immigrants to fill jobs the Germans did not want, after the unification, Germans are finding jobs scarce. Foreigners who are seen as competition for jobs, housing, and welfare money are the most obvious symbols and targets of the young Germans' frustration. In 1992 alone, there were 2,285 attacks against foreign asylum seekers in Germany, mostly perpetrated by young neo-Nazi skinheads wearing Nazi armbands, swastikas, and steel-toed boots and executing stiff-armed salutes.

ATTACKS ON THE HANDICAPPED

Although most of the skinhead attacks are directed against immigrants, handicapped people have been targeted as well. There is a growing concern among the handicapped that the neo-Nazis view them as an economic burden to the country. "They just attack us now," said one 66-year-old man who is bound to a wheelchair. "From there it's not very far to talk about euthanasia."

> A 25-year-old man who has been bound to a wheelchair all his life found himself surrounded by skinheads as he shopped in his hometown of Cologne. As they encircled him, they shouted, "They must have forgotten you in Dachau." Fortunately, other shoppers saw what was happening and came to his rescue, positioning themselves between him and the skins.

The number of attacks for 1992 cited above does not include attacks against handicapped people.

IGNORANCE OF THE PAST

Estimates run as high as 50,000 right-wingers in Germany, most influenced by the Nazi philosophy and a belief that they are fighting for what is right for their country. About 70 percent of the skins are younger than 20 years of age, and some, called "baby skins," are no older than 12.

In eastern Germany, the young neo-Nazis have no knowledge of their own history because the Communist regime distorted the teachings in school. West Germany spent the years since World War II practicing something called *bewaltigung der vergangenheit*, translated to mean "coming to terms with or mastering the [Nazi] past." The former East Germany, however, did not make the same effort; instead it attempted to just forget the horrific past. The result is that nearly three generations of East Germans grew up either ignorant of their country's past or with a completely distorted view of it. But many old-timers have not forgotten and see today's violence as a repeat of the early days of Nazi Germany. "The Holocaust began a half-century ago the same way as things are happening now," one Jewish resident of Germany said.

> Skinhead attacks against Vietnamese and Mozambicans became so intense that the police had to move the foreigners to military camps. Old Germans, who watched grimly as the people were hustled into the camps, said, "You have only to add the German shepherds and the watchtowers, and the concentration camp is perfect."

CITIZEN SUPPORT OF THE SKINHEADS

The young neo-Nazi street thugs have the sympathy of many people in the mainstream, including some of the police.

> As nearly 800 police officers battled with 500 neo-Nazi skinheads who were armed with stones

HE LIVES!

Hitler is still worshipped by neo-Nazi skinheads everywhere.

and firebombs, hundreds of locals cheered on the skins. Then when the skinheads attacked 200 Rumanian refugees, the citizens again cheered the neo-Nazis and deliberately interfered with the police. "We want the same thing as the young Nazis," said one elderly observer. "To get rid of them."

Although thousands of Germans have protested in the streets against the right-wing violence, while others held vigils in front of refugee shelters, a recent poll showed that a third of the German population sympathized with the skinheads and believed the Nazi era had some positive points. A whopping 96 percent of those polled were opposed to Germany accepting any more refugees.

The Associated Press found in a survey that out of 16 homicides by neo-Nazis in 1992, fewer than half resulted in convictions. Critics say Germany's justice system frees neo-Nazis just hours after they are arrested, releasing them for yet another round of attacks.

THE LEFT-WINGERS

Adding to the insanity of the situation in cities like Hamburg and Berlin, left-wing anarchists, Germans violently opposed to the violence the neo-Nazi skinheads are inflicting on refugees, frequently fight against the skins using knives, bats, and arson. It's not uncommon for the leftists to kill and inflict many injuries in their fight to stop the violence.

THE VIOLENCE GOES ON

Although the German government has banned Nazi regalia and several right-wing organizations, the violence has continued.

In the northern city of Brandenburg, police arrested two skinheads for murder after they doused a man with gasoline and set him ablaze.

•

On a road near Berlin, a group of skinheads in cars rammed two other cars containing refugees. When the cars were forced to stop, the skins attacked them with clubs.

•

Thousands of skinheads marched in Rudolstadt, shouting, "Remember the dead," as they demonstrated in honor of the death of Nazi deputy Rudolf Hess. Police arrested 170 skins for rioting.

•

Police fired warning shots in the air in Wismar in an attempt to stop the fighting between Germans and foreigners.

Germany is not the only European county to suffer from neo-Nazi violence. The sickness is spreading to countries like France, Spain, Australia, and Austria, where racist graffiti, protests, harassment, and gatherings take place with crowds of right-wingers numbering more than 10,000.

KEEP AN EAR TO THEIR MUSIC

It's also important that we pay attention to the music American skinheads listen to because much of it's imported from Europe.

> "We fight shaved, our fists are hard as steel,
> Our hearts beat true for our Fatherland.
> Whatever may happen, we will never leave you,
> We will stand true for our Germany,
> Because we are the strength for Germany,
> That makes Germany clean.
> Germany Awake!"

"Germany Awake!" is a slogan the Nazis used during their rise to power in the early 1930s. When white-power bands sing it in a concert, a thousand German neo-Nazi skinheads snap to attention, chanting "Sieg Heil," and rhythmically snap their arms out in stiff-armed salutes.

Nazi regalia remains popular even though it's been banned by the German government.

Someone unfurls a black-white-and-red Third Reich battle flag emblazoned with the swastika.

This is heady stuff for German skinheads and for American skinheads here too. Our skins do some of the same antics at concerts and rallies as are done in Germany. They learn it from the media and from traveling to Europe, and they see the pictures on the album covers of the European Oi music they so covet.

SIMILARITIES TO AMERICA

Although events are happening on a much larger scale in Europe, the same things its skinheads oppose—minorities, homosexuals, handicapped, and government money going to minorities in the form of welfare, food

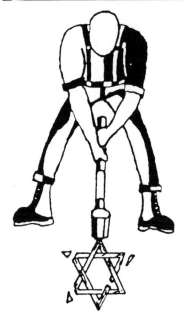

stamps, and housing—are things racist skinheads here object to.

There is equal concern in both Europe and America about right-wing extremists entering the political arena and the support they get from quiet voters. Of equal concern is violence by left-wing anti-racists.

The enormity of the situation in Germany and in other European countries creates international press coverage, exciting film footage that American skinheads watch on the six o'clock news. When our skinheads see what is happening in the country where it all began, it energizes them. It gives validity to what they are doing here.

CHAPTER 15

As mentioned earlier, skinhead gangs, all gangs for that matter, are not made up of special beings from another planet. There are, however, specific nuances to each gang—white, Hispanic, black, Asian, and all gangs in between—that will influence how you deal with them tactically in high-risk situations. The knowledge you have acquired from this text will help you understand the nuances indigenous to the skinhead culture. Let's take a look at a few specific tactics that should be used when confronting skinheads in high-risk situations.

KEEP IN MIND WHERE THEIR MINDS ARE

Most of the time, you do not know what or whom you have when you stop a car or approach a person on the sidewalk. The man looking out of place on the corner may have just chain-sawed his entire family into cordwood, or it may be that he is just new in town and confused about the bus schedule. Although the same unknown elements exist when you approach one or more skinheads, there are a few specifics about them that you can assume.

At the top of the list is the basic fact that racist or antiracist skinheads do not like you. The racist

TACTICS

skins view you as part of the ZOG they believe is involved in a giant conspiracy to oppress the white working class. To them you are a gun-toting puppet, the military arm of the Jewish subjugators. To the antiracist skins, you are just as bad as the neo-Nazis and the Ku Klux Klan; in fact, since you are a police officer, you probably associate with one or more white supremacy organizations. They too see you as an oppressor, part of a racist government that is continually holding down—indeed killing—minorities, homosexuals, the poor, etc.

It's also important to remember that many, if not all, skinhead gang members are antiauthority and violence-prone. Your crisp uniform, shiny badge, and creaking leather symbolize the oppression both factions believe they are struggling under. You are much more visible than that seemingly invisible giant power in some far-off, marble-pillared building. You are right there in front of them, representing all that they hate. You are the closest one they can get.

Two uniformed officers responded to a domestic violence call where a skinhead had assaulted his girlfriend. When the two officers arrived, they found the 6-foot, 210-pound skinhead in the backyard. The officers advised him he was under arrest, with each taking an arm, but neither applying a control hold.

The skin immediately broke away, knocked the taller officer to the ground, and jumped on him. As he mauled the officer, the second officer struck the skin over two dozen times with his PR-24.

When the officers attempted to handcuff him, the skinhead broke away, and once more the shorter officer repeatedly struck him with his PR-24. When the officer grew fatigued, he tossed his stick to his partner, who had lost his in the fight. The taller officer then took his turn delivering blows to the seemingly invulnerable skinhead, who eventually backed off a few feet and challenged the officers to continue the fight.

The two tired officers held their ground, anxiously waiting for code-three backup to arrive.

But before it got there, the skin charged, pushed the taller officer off a three-foot-high retaining wall, leaped down on him, and continued his mad assault, breaking the officer's nose, lacerating his mouth, and giving him internal injuries.

Only after additional officers struck him with their PR-24s were they able to apply handcuffs and finally gain control of him.

Skinheads and white supremacists are in possession of weapons more now than ever before. The last 10 years of the white supremacy movement in the United States is replete with shootouts between law enforcement and white supremacists. Virtually all these incidents have been made into movies for the big screen and for television. Although the bad guys always lose in the end, their effort and even their demise are seen by some racist skinheads as glorious. Indeed, many of them have great fantasies of blazing shootouts with ZOG. Some even follow a religion that teaches it's a sin to give in to the evil government.

When skinheads are demonstrating together, say in front of a courthouse or an abortion clinic, they feel powerful. It's the simple psychology of unity, strength in numbers, a sense of family, and a feeling of "us versus them." As a result of this augmented power, skinheads are more likely to verbally harass and physically resist you.

FIELD INTERROGATION

Skinheads will act out when they think they are free to do so. One way in which gangs get a foothold in a community is when their presence is ignored or denied, thus allowing them to roam freely and to break the law. It's incumbent upon you to find, stop, and talk with skinheads. Putting it another way, it's important that you "get in their face" whenever the opportunity presents itself.

Let's say that as you are patrolling in a car or on foot, you observe four skinheads standing in front of a convenience store. Whether you recognize one of them as a wanted subject, you have reason to believe one or more of them has committed a crime, or you simply want to engage them in conversation, your approach and contact should be done with utmost safety. Before you do anything, consider these facts:

- Shootings often occur during field interrogations.
- Most shootings occur when officers are within close range of the suspect.
- Field interrogations often deteriorate to physical encounters.
- Skinheads do not like the police.
- If you are a minority officer, your risk level is higher.
- More and more skinheads are carrying weapons.
- Skinheads are braver when there are two or more together.
- Skinheads are more likely to put on a show if there are citizens in the area.

As you observe them for a few minutes, ask yourself these questions:

1. How many are there?
2. Do you know any of them?
3. If you know them, what do you know about them?
   —Propensity to carry weapons
   —Wanted status
   —Parole or probation restrictions
   —Mental stability
   —Past history
   —Past relationship with you
4. Are they new to you? If so, are they local? Are they from out of town? Do you recognize their patches? Do they have backpacks or anything else that indicates they are new in town?
5. Whether they are new or not, how do they act when they see you?
6. Do any of them look like they are going to run?
7. Are there any vehicles that belong to them?

8. Are there any visible weapons—knife in boot, baseball bat, chain hanging from a belt, walking cane?

Visually scan them from head to foot. If their heads are freshly shaved and their boots highly polished, you can assume they are very much involved in the skinhead movement. If there is some kind of an event happening soon, such as a concert, rally, or demonstration, they are going to be psyched, and the risk level of your contact will be higher.

Look to see if they are trying to hide something. When they see you, do they shuffle around as if to conceal a baseball bat leaning against the wall? Do they appear to be handing something off, throwing something away, dropping something behind them? Does one of them hold his arm stiffly, as if something were up his sleeve? Look for arms that are pressed against the sides of jackets, an indicator that a weapon may be in the waistband.

> Suspicious that a skinhead was carrying a weapon in a shoulder holster, an officer secured the skin's arms and reached inside his flight jacket. The officer did find a shoulder holster, but riding in the pouch was a very large, very alive rat.

Before you make a move in their direction, tell dispatch where you are, what you are going to do, and the make, model, and license plate of the skins' vehicle. Ask for backup, even if you and your partner have worked together like a well-made watch for years. Given the mentality of skinheads, it's too risky for two officers to deal with four or even three of them.

Your next thought is where and how you are going to confront them. As with any approach, you try to choose the best location, a place that benefits you and, in the event the situation deteriorates and hits the proverbial fan, is safest for nearby citizens. For example, if the skins are standing in front of a convenience market, you would want to maneuver them around to the side of the store where there is less vehicular and foot traffic. One way to manage this would be to approach them near the store's corner and direct them around to the side. If you can only approach from the front of the store, use the ruse that you do not want to interfere with the customers, so let's all move around to the side. If you are downtown in a busy shopping area, plan your approach away from heavy pedestrian traffic, such as theaters, restaurants, and stores. You want to make your contact where there are few people, not only for the safety of the citizens, but also to reduce the chance of their interference.

You may find that you have to wait awhile before you make your approach. If the skinheads are standing in front of a theater and show no indication of moving, you should wait until the ticket rush is over before you approach them. If the skins are in a place with a never-ending flow of citizens, you just might have to wait until they move on their own. If you are in a car, you will have to sit down the street and wait. If you are on foot, you will have to pretend to be busy as you wait until the opportunity presents itself to make your approach.

MAKING CONTACT

If you and your cover are on foot, it's best to approach from oblique angles. This makes it difficult for the skins to flee and is also psychologically disconcerting to them because they are forced to divide their attention. Watch for danger signals as you make your approach, such as:

- A sense of panic on one or more of the skinheads' faces
- A furtive move toward the inside of a jacket
- A preparatory move as if to run
- An attempt by one or more of the skins to conceal something
- Any posturing that indicates a fight
- Splitting up

Stop no closer than three feet away and watch their

hands. Stand at an oblique angle in a stable stance, your gun side away, ready to move quickly in any direction. If it appears that the skinheads are playing off each other, split them up, your cover watching two of them a few feet away, and you and another officer taking the other two. If there are only two skins and you and another officer are making the contact, you talk with one while the other officer talks to the second skin a short distance away. If there are three skins, two officers will talk to two, and a third officer will get the remaining one.

Do not allow the skinheads to move into your three-foot safety range. Remember the principal: *Action is faster than reaction.* If the subject gets within your safety space and decides to punch you, you will not be able to react in time. Maintain a distance greater than three feet to allow yourself reaction time, and keep your attention focused on the skinheads.

WHEN ONE OR MORE SKINHEADS ARE ARMED

Let's say you are in a two-person car and dispatch informs you there is an armed skinhead standing in front of a restaurant. You need to choose an approach site that is away from citizens and that offers you good cover, something that will stop a bullet. A tree branch with lots of leaves will conceal you but probably will not stop a round. Telephone poles are good cover, as well as mail boxes and door insets. Your car door is not bad, but your fender, wheel well, hood, and trunk are better. You want a solid place of cover where you can draw your weapon and order the skinhead to comply with your commands.

Since foot traffic is heavy, find a location where you can watch the suspect and wait until the sidewalk clears. Or, you may choose to wait until he moves away from the restaurant to an area where there are fewer citizens. Either plan is appropriate; your choice will be dependent on whatever extenuating factors exist.

If you have to approach in your car, keep your eyes on the skinhead as you pull up, centering the front end of your car on him. If you are alone in your car, you should stop at an angle so the threat will be on the other side of the hood, providing you some degree of cover. In a situation where there are two people in the car, you want to center the threat so you are not exposing your partner. Depending on the situation, there are a number of approaches available to you:

1. You can use the car doors for cover (bullets can penetrate car doors and be skipped on pavement into your shins).
2. You can move quickly to a better source of cover, such as a post or side of a building.
3. You can push the doors open with your feet so you can stay seated and use the window frame to brace your weapon.
4. You can simply get out and walk up to the skinhead.

Another tactic is to approach on foot. If you are working by yourself, *make sure backup has been dispatched, and wait for it*, even if you are close to the call. Meet the backup a block away or around the corner and decide how you are going to approach the skinhead.

Let's say you and your backup decide to walk down the sidewalk, pretending to casually stroll by the skinhead. If he sees the two of you, pretend to pay him no special attention, *though you are constantly aware of where his hands are and where available cover is*. If he nods, speaks, or asks the time, take advantage of the moment by quickly moving in on him. If he does not see your approach or ignores you by keeping his back turned as you pass, take him.

Each of you should move in simultaneously, grab an arm, and apply a control hold. Immediately handcuff and search him. Ask him if he is carrying a weapon. Most skinheads will tell you they have a gun, figuring you will probably find it anyway. But if you do not ask and you miss it during the search, the skin will not volunteer to correct your error.

When there are two or three skinheads and one is reported to be armed, approach with three officers. Be cognizant so as to avoid a crossfire situation and be aware of available cover. Only one officer should give the commands, using a strong, authoritative voice to order their hands up, to turn around slowly, and to interlace their fingers behind their heads. Let them know you have reason to believe that one or more of them may be armed. It's a judgment call whether you and the other officers have your hands on the butts of your holstered weapons or have your weapons drawn.

If there are four officers and four skinheads, order the skins to line up side by side, with enough space in between them so they cannot hand off a weapon. Then, two officers will conduct a two-on-one search, as the other officers observe the remaining three. If there are two officers and two suspects, each officer will search one. In the event of a high-risk situation, one officer will search while the second officer observes both his partner's search and the second skinhead. It's your choice whether you use a standing, kneeling, or prone search position. Keep in mind, however, that while standing is fine, kneeling is even stronger, and prone is the strongest of all.

If you find that the skins are not armed, offer an apology and engage them in conversation. If they are angry about the search, you probably will not get much out of them. They may even file a complaint.

Let them. You acted on information given to you. You can articulate that skinheads are known gang members who have an international history of violence. They have a propensity for carrying weapons and for hating the government in general, law enforcement agencies in particular.

Do not let the possibility of a complaint ever deter you from using good officer survival tactics. Would you rather have to explain your actions to an internal affairs investigator or have six of your buddies carry your coffin?

TRAFFIC STOPS

As mentioned elsewhere, skinheads usually drive old beaters, although occasionally one will have his parents' new station wagon or four-wheel drive. You can presume that skinheads' proficiency behind the wheel and their inclination to have a driver's license and registration are no different from that of the rest of the motoring public. But you cannot presume anything on a traffic stop. Even when you have previous information on the vehicle and its occupants, it's still dangerous to make presumptions. You just might be wrong.

> Two officers were staking out a convenience store, watching for an older white car that was being driven by an armed skinhead who was coming to shoot a gang rival. The officers spotted a white Pontiac pass through the lot; except for longer hair, its driver matched the description. The officers pulled the car over a block away.
>
> As the officers walked up on either side of the car, the driver officer immediately saw that the person behind the wheel was not the suspect they were looking for. Assuming the driver was just a Joe Blow citizen, the officer waved off his partner, who returned to the police car. The driver officer relaxed, looked around at passing cars and pedestrians, and joked with the driver as he waited for the routine check to come back from dispatch. A few minutes later, dispatch relayed that the man was in fact a documented skinhead, affiliated with a violent, police-hating white supremacy gang. A subsequent search disclosed weapons in the car and on the skinhead, who just coincidentally was in the area and had nothing to do with the other skinhead the officers were looking for.

Although not every skinhead vehicle will contain a firearm, you will almost always find some kind of a clubbing device (e.g., bat, pipe, police baton, chain). Therefore, no matter what the initial violation, every traffic stop should be conducted with caution and proper tactics.

The moment you begin thinking about stopping the vehicle, you need to *assess the risk:*

- What was the violation or what was it that drew your attention to the vehicle? The traffic violation may have been only "interfering with traffic," but it involved the car sitting in the intersection as one of the occupants, a skinhead, brandished a bat out the window at a Chinese pedestrian.
- How many occupants are in the vehicle? Now that you know the mind-set of skinheads, you know the danger potential to you is proportional to the number of skins.
- How are the skinheads behaving? Are they doing a lot of twisting and turning when you pull in behind them? When you activate your lights, do they look as if they are reaching under the seats? Are they jockeying as if to get in a better position? Does the driver pull off a busy street onto a uninhabited one? Do they all get out when you make the stop?
- Do you know before you make the stop if they have weapons? Is there a rifle in the truck gun rack, a bat in the back window? Can you see a weapon as you walk up on the vehicle? Does one or more of the occupants get out with a weapon?
- What type of vehicle is involved? A windowless van presents a different challenge than a sedan does. A pickup with a legal rifle in the gun rack requires a different plan than a motorcycle does.
- What is the setting of your stop? Is the driver pulling over where he wants rather than where you want him to? Is he pulling in front of his house where there are more skins inside?
- What do you have in your favor? Are you carrying a five-shot Chief's Special or an 18-shot Glock? Are you a one-person or two-person car? How far off is your backup? Does the setting provide good cover for you? Do you know any of the occupants?

You need to make these risk assessments in a matter of

seconds to decide on your tactical strategy. Keep in mind that even when you decide on a plan, you may have to change it suddenly. The situation may be worse than you thought initially, and you need to switch gears quickly. It's rather like an officer trying to apply a wrist flex and continuing to try to make it work even when the suspect is throwing him all about.

When the situation changes and your initial plan is no longer apropos, then you have to move to plan B. But before you change plans, you have to determine that plan A no longer applies. Those officers who do not see the need for a backup plan often get hurt. Keep your eyes and your mind open so you can change your tactics instantly.

Points to keep in mind specific to skinheads:

- Given the skinhead mind-set, a vehicle with only one skinhead should be considered a moderate- to high-risk stop.
- Since skinheads get most of their power, strength, and bravado from their gang, two or more skinheads in a car should be considered as high risk.
- *Always* call for backup no matter how many occupants there are.
- Throughout your contact, maintain a tactical advantage. Begin by positioning your vehicle so as to provide you safety and cover. Your backup should position their vehicles with the same tactics in mind.
- If it's a moderate- to high-risk stop and you choose to walk up on them, do so only with another officer on the other side of the suspect vehicle. Order the occupants to place their hands on the front windows or the roof. Visually scan the interior for weapons in laps, on the seats, dash, floor, or anywhere to which the skins would have quick and easy access. If there are no passengers in the backseat, position yourself behind the driver's door so you can see in and the driver has to twist around to see you. Get his license and return to your car to conduct your checks and write the citation.
- If the stop is extremely high risk, use your PA system

to order the occupants out one at a time. Make them walk backward to a safe zone by the police cars where other officers will conduct the searching and hand-cuffing. Continue this process until all the skinheads are out of the car. Keep them separated to reduce their psychological strength.

- *Always* search the occupants. They are gang members with a history of carrying weapons. If the passengers feel you are violating their rights because you only stopped the driver for not activating his turn signal, so be it. Better to go home in one piece and be alive to answer their complaints tomorrow.
- Ask the driver permission to search the vehicle if you do not have a legal right to do so. That way if you find contraband, you can legally seize it and make an arrest. If you find a clubbing device, you can seize it for safekeeping, given skinhead's history of using clubs to assault people.

Officers are killed every year conducting traffic stops. The potential for your getting hurt exists on every stop you make. When the occupants are skinheads, a gang with a history of hate, violence, and an antigovernment and antiauthority philosophy, the risk goes up even more. It's imperative, therefore, that you stay alert and exercise extreme caution as you employ the best tactics for the situation.

SKINHEAD PARTIES

Getting dispatched to a loud skinhead party at a house or apartment is a high-risk call with lots of potential for problems. Keep these risk factors in mind:

- The skinheads will feel strength and courage because of their numbers.
- When you show up you will be representing the government that both racist and antiracist skins so vehemently despise.

- Heavy drinking will give them even more bravado.
- There is a high probability there will be weapons on the premises.
- Quite likely, there will be skinheads present who have wants and warrants.
- Minority officers may be at greater risk because of the skinheads' crowd mentality.

There are three basic reasons why you would get a radio call to a skinhead party: 1) information has been received that a wanted person is at the location; 2) complaints of noise and rowdy behavior from neighbors; and 3) someone has reported a crime, such as an assault. There are several ways to handle any one of these calls. Let's examine some methods that have worked well for other officers.

If you get information that a wanted person is at a skinhead party, you have to decide how important the warrant and the skinhead are, given the risk factor of going in after him. If the warrant is for theft or traffic, you may want to consider arresting him at a later date or waiting down the street for him to leave.

On the other hand, you may want to use the minor warrant as an excuse to go into the party to see who is there and what is going on. Although the warrant will legally allow you to get in, gather intelligence, and check other skins for wants and warrants, keep in mind that the effort may require a dozen or more officers. This is an important consideration if manpower is low and the shift is a busy one.

However, if the warrant is significant—robbery, serious assault, rape, murder—it will have to be served. Now your options are fewer: wait outside for him to come out or go in and get him.

When You Have to Go to the Party

If you get a radio call to a skinhead party concerning loud music, drunken behavior, or a serious crime, you will have to respond to the complaint rather than wait it out. Your first step will be to decide how to do so tactically. First, you must take into consideration what you know about the situation:

- How many skinheads are at the party?
- What do you know about specific individuals in attendance, particularly dangerous individuals?
- What information do you have about weapons?
- Is the party at a house or an apartment?
- What is the setting?
    —Proximity to other houses or apartments
    —Lighting, foliage, parked cars, skinheads outside
    —How visible are you when you approach?
    —Is there a backyard, alleyway, fence, wall?
    —Are there illegally parked vehicles?

Once you have answered these questions as well as you can, consider how many officers you need and how you will employ them.

One sure way to get skinheads out of a house quickly is to start towing their illegally parked cars. Serving the warrant will also get the others to come out. A third way is to arrest one or more skins who have spilled outside from the party. You can usually get them for public drinking, underage drinking, or some kind of disorderly con-

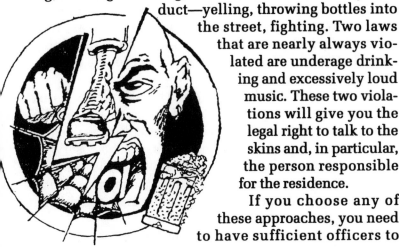

duct—yelling, throwing bottles into the street, fighting. Two laws that are nearly always violated are underage drinking and excessively loud music. These two violations will give you the legal right to talk to the skins and, in particular, the person responsible for the residence.

If you choose any of these approaches, you need to have sufficient officers to handle all the skinheads who will most assuredly pour out of the house to see what is going on and display their disapproval.

Obviously 10 skinheads will be easier to handle than 50. But no matter how many there are, you need to control and watch them every second you are dealing with them. When they come out of the house or the apartment into the yard or parking lot, you will want officers to search them and other officers to watch the searching process. Or if you are serving a warrant, you may just want to grab the wanted skin, rush him to the car, and get out of the area without dealing with the others.

Loud Party Call

Let's say you respond to a large-party call where the majority of skinheads are outside in the yard or driveway. If there are no extenuating circumstances for you to order everyone to the ground, you are probably going to search them in a standing position.

Line the skinheads up with enough space them between so they are unable to hand anything off to each other. Some officers have them face a wall to reduce their ability to escape. This is tactically permissible as long as you do not have them lean against the wall, a dangerous position because they can push off and spin around on you.

Either one officer will search, or two officers will, using a two-on-one method. One or two officers will watch the search while the others monitor the remaining skins in the line. If the situation is volatile, the officers should have their batons at the ready.

If a searcher finds a weapon, he should call out "Knife!" or "Gun!" so the other officers are aware. The skinhead should then be arrested, handcuffed, walked to a police car, and secured in the backseat. The observing officers continue to watch the unsearched skins until the searching officers return. Or if there are enough officers, one or two more can move up to the line and begin searching the next skin.

When you have brought the situation to some kind of

a conclusion but you do not have a legal right to go into the house or apartment, ask permission to do so. You probably will be told no, but you may be told yes. If you can get in, it's a great opportunity to look around and gather as much intelligence as you can.

Serious Assault Call

You can legally go into the house or apartment if there has been a report of a crime, such as a shooting, stabbing, or serious assault. It's important to keep in mind that the collective energy of all the skinheads, combined with alcohol consumption and their elevated emotional level brought on by the violence, will add up to a volatile, high-risk situation.

Do not go inside until you have sufficient cover. If you are the first to arrive, stay back a block or more and advise dispatch of your location so your backup can meet you. If it's a shooting or stabbing call, ask dispatch if an ambulance has been dispatched. If so, you may want to consider having the ambulance meet you first. In many jurisdictions, ambulance companies will not go to a shooting call without police backup anyway.

Although it is rarely available, you would like to have as much information as possible before you go to the scene, including:

- How many skinheads are at the party?
- Where did the shooting or assault occur?
  —Inside the premises
  —In the yard or in the driveway
- Where is the perpetrator?
- Where is the victim?
- Does the perpetrator still have the weapon?

Dispatch should have automatically asked those questions when they received the call. If they did not, ask them to call back and get it. If they cannot get any additional information, then you will have to go in with what you have.

If the victim is in the yard, most of the skinheads will

be outside. You should approach on foot from at least a half block away so you can see what is going on. Ensure that your backup is not moving into a crossfire position.

Let's say you see someone down on the ground and there are several skinheads standing about. Given everything you know about skinheads and the instability of the situation, you do not want to rush in. From a position of cover, identify yourself as the police and order the skinheads into the prone position. Backup officers should also be behind cover and spread out on either side of you. *Watch the skinheads' hands.*

If you know one of the skinheads by name, or one is easily identifiable, call out to him. For example, "Basher" or "You without a shirt on." Then ask, "Where is the shooter? Where is the gun now? How badly is your buddy hurt?"

If the shooter identifies himself and admits to having the gun in his possession, order him to crawl to your location. If he has it in his hand, order him to drop it. If it's in his pocket, do not tell him to reach in and remove it. You do not want him to touch it. Make it clear to him that if he attempts to go for the weapon, he will most definitely be shot. Two or three officers should cover him at gunpoint as he moves toward you, while the other officers watch the remaining skins. Once he has moved to where you want him, one or two officers should take control. They will then order him to crawl behind cover so they can search and handcuff him out of the line of fire of any other skinhead who may be armed.

It's dangerous to have an armed skinhead behind cover with you, but he will be covered by at least two police weapons as he lies on his belly. This is safer than searching a subject in the open.

Once the shooter has been secured, ask the remaining skinheads if any of them are carrying weapons. If two or three say they are carrying—and like other criminals they often admit it—order each one, one at a time, to crawl to your location. Handcuff and search each one.

You have first dealt with the skinheads who have admitted they are armed. Since the remaining skins may or may not be telling the truth, order them, one at a time, to crawl over to you and proceed with them as you did with the others. If some of them refuse to move, you will have to go to them. When you leave your position of cover, keep your firearm trained on the threat. If you are going to be the searcher, two officers should move out with you. Two of the officers still behind cover will train their weapons on the house, which has yet to be cleared, while the remaining officers watch the unsearched prone skins.

Move to the closest skinhead and holster your weapon while the other two officers cover him with their weapons. Search and handcuff. As you get him to his feet and begin to move him toward cover, the two cover officers will go with you, moving backward, their weapons trained on the unsearched skinheads. Hand him off to the officers behind cover, then the three of you move back out and repeat the process with the next skinhead.

Although there are other effective methods that can be used, the bottom line is that at the scene of a shooting, where there are multiple skinheads, you and the other officers do not want to go wading into them before they have been searched. The fact there has been a shooting or a knifing clearly indicates that the situation was out of control before your arrival. You need to establish control as quickly as you can for the safety of the police, any onlookers, and the skinheads—in that order. Stay behind cover; take your time; be safe.

The situation is potentially more dangerous if the

shooting has taken place inside the dwelling and the victim, the shooter, and all the other skinheads are still inside. Before you go in, consider these questions:

- How many people are inside?
- Do I have information that the shooter has already left?
- Did the call come from someone inside? From a neighbor?
- Can dispatch call back and tell the shooter to come out with his hands in the air?
- If the victim is mobile, can dispatch tell him to come out?
- Are there skinheads outside the dwelling with whom I can communicate?
- What is the physical setting?
  —How many doors?
  —How many windows?
  —What is its proximity to other houses or apartments?
  —Are there press and onlookers present?
  —How many officers are available for the job?

The best scenario is to have dispatch make contact with the occupants and tell the shooter to come out the door with his hands up. From a position of cover, you can then order him to stop and then turn around slowly so you can visually check for weapons. Order the other skinheads to stay back, then tell the shooter to advance slowly to your location. Once he is within a few feet, tell him to turn around and back toward your voice. This position provides you with a little more reaction time should he decide to go for a gun and turn back toward you. Once he has moved to a place you deem safe to search and handcuff, order him to the ground. Ask him if any of his buddies have weapons, then ask about the condition of the victim and where he is in the house.

If dispatch cannot make contact with anyone within the house, or the shooter refuses to come out, you have a choice of either waiting him out or going in after him. If you wait him out, you will need to set up a perimeter, call for a supervisor, remove any neighbors who may be in danger, and try to establish telephonic contact with him.

It's true you need to be concerned about the shooting victim, but you also need to think about the safety of yourself and your fellow officers. It will not do the shooting victim any good if officers get shot rushing into the house prematurely.

Going into a house or apartment full of skinheads who have been drinking, who may be armed with anything from knives to stolen military weapons, and where someone has already been shot is a job best suited for a police SWAT team. Establish cover and your perimeter, clear out the neighbors, and call SWAT.

On a physical assault call, usually the result of a fight, you will have to go into the dwelling to check on the victim and arrest the perpetrator. The suspect may be just inside the door, hiding in the basement, or secreted in the attic. The other skinheads may stand by while you search, or they may try to interfere. Since you may encounter an infinite number of variables inside the dwelling, you will want to employ enough officers to do the job safely.

If there are 30 skinheads inside, you should use 15 to 20 officers—more if they are available. Three or four officers should be stationed at the rear of the dwelling, setting themselves up so they can watch the structure's rear as well as its sides. At least one officer should remain with the vehicles to safeguard them against vandalism.

> In one beachside resort community, several officers were contacting a group of skinheads inside a video arcade. While their police cars sat unattended, a skinhead duck-walked from police car to police car plunging a knife into the tires.

So they cannot later say that they did not know you were the police, identify yourself as a police officer to the person at the door, even when you are in uniform. Tell him you have received information that someone is hurt inside. If it looks as if he is going to deny you entry, ask to talk with the owner or the person on the lease. Tell that person you have a report that a serious crime has been committed on the premises and you need to come in to investigate. If the owner allows you to enter, your legal position will be stronger if the entry becomes an issue in court. If he says "No," you will have to use the necessary force to gain entry since you are obligated to check for an injured person.

When you move in, do so quickly, while remaining alert and watching their hands carefully. Only two officers should make the physical arrest while the other officers watch the other skins. Remember: 1) the skinheads will not have been searched; 2) there is a high probability of weapons in the house; and 3) alcohol consumption and their sense of unity will have given them a strong sense of courage.

If the victim and perpetrator are in one room, keep the other skinheads away. Do not let their taunts bait you into a verbal or physical confrontation. Your job is to get the victim and the perpetrator and move out quickly. The job of the other officers is to keep the skinheads back so the suspect and victim can be removed safely and quickly.

If you need to interview witnesses, do so as soon as the suspect and victim have been removed from the area. Skinheads will be more likely to talk to you immediately after an incident than later after they have had time to talk to their buddies. Separate them as you usually do, and then have one or two officers conduct the interviews while the other officers provide security.

When dealing with a crowd of skins, especially outdoors, you need to watch everyone carefully, especially people in the back and out on the periphery. Watch for thrown missiles—bottles, cans, lawn chairs, rocks.

> As four officers attempted to take an antiracist skinhead into custody, other antiracists threw rocks, bricks, flower planters, and soda cans. The crowd grabbed at the officers' service weapons, batons, car keys, and made attempts to pull the prisoner away from them.

ROCK CONCERTS AND DEMONSTRATIONS

Although rock concerts and demonstrations are generally unrelated, they present situations that require basically the same police tactics. Their dynamics involve large numbers of people, most of whom will not be skinheads but are either sympathizers or people diametrically opposed to their philosophy.

Additionally, you will be dealing with a lot of people who do not like you and all that you represent. A concert, for example, will draw hundreds if not thousands of young people, but only a few dozen skinheads. The skins will dislike you for all the reasons mentioned before, and many of the other young people will dislike you simply because you represent authority. On the happy side, however, there will be many who will be supportive and even cheer as you remove skinhead troublemakers.

Racist skinhead demonstrations will usually be small in number, but the people opposed to the demonstration will be many times larger and always cause the most problems. Antiracist skinheads sometimes demonstrate by themselves, but usually join forces with left-wing groups to oppose some perceived injustice. When these groups turn violent, antiracist skinheads will be your greatest problem.

> A group of 1,000 protesters gathered in the town center to protest the first Rodney King verdict. At one point, 200 unruly demonstrators broke away from the others and moved to the police station to gather and decide what to do. Three antiracist skinheads climbed atop statues, each shouting for the attention of the crowd. One wanted to storm the police station, another wanted to turn around and attack the police line that was forming behind them, and the third wanted to run down the street and break store windows. The crowd went with the latter, but their rampage was short as the police moved in quickly to control them.

When dealing with dangerous crowds, you want to stay on the periphery, always cognizant of your back.

> At a racist skinhead demonstration in California, the police found themselves trapped

> between skinheads to their front and anarchists
> who were taking advantage of the situation to their
> rear. Before it was over, several police officers
> received injuries from thrown objects, including
> cans, rocks, garbage cans, and a park bench.

Never let anyone get behind you. It's a bad sandwich when you are the ingredients.

When you see someone in a crowd commit a crime or violation (e.g., using a megaphone without a permit or throwing a paint-filled balloon), you do not always have to act immediately, especially if the crowd far outnumbers the police. Wait until later to make the arrest so you have the advantage: the crowd thins; the suspect traps himself between two cars; he moves close to the police line.

Never go into the crowd with fewer than six to 10 officers. Move in quickly and surround the perpetrator. Only two officers will make the arrest, while the others provide a circle of security, their backs to the arrest team, their fronts facing the crowd.

The crowd will taunt you and may advance on you, but do not break your security formation. Your job at the moment is to protect your arrest team while their focus is on the suspect. If you see another person break the law, note it in your mind but wait until later to get him. If someone advances on you as if to hurt you or free the suspect, maintain your position and use your baton only when he is within your striking range. One more time: *Do not go after him; maintain your position.*

Once the suspect is handcuffed, the arrest team walks him out of the crowd while the other officers walk on each side of them to provide security. Get the arrestee out of the area as quickly as possible since his presence in handcuffs will rile the crowd.

> A sergeant ordered his squad of eight officers to
> move into a hostile crowd of antiracist skins and
> other left-wing protesters to arrest a man using a
> megaphone. Two officers quickly handcuffed the
> man as the other officers surrounded the arrest

team in a tight security formation. But as the squad began to move out of the crowd, a big antiracist pushed one of the officers in the chest. The officer dumped the man onto the pavement and began to grapple with him. Because of the crowd noise and the confusion, only one other officer saw the scuffle and stopped to help make the arrest.

Without a security formation, the crowd was able to rush in and strike the arresting officers with sticks and protest signs. Luckily, the officers were wearing riot helmets and were able to tolerate the blows and get the man handcuffed and onto his feet. Then, creating a path with their pepper Mace, the officers worked their way out of the crowd.

Be aware of one negative aspect of waiting until a later time to arrest someone out of the crowd. When you wait perhaps 15 minutes, the dynamics of the crowd may change. That is, some of the people may move down the street to where something else is going on, and new people may join the crowd you are monitoring. Many of them will be unaware that someone in the crowd committed a crime a few minutes earlier. So when you and several other uniform officers suddenly move into their midst and take a person into custody, the others see it as the oppressive government arbitrarily picking someone out of their midst for arrest. This perception often causes a wave of resistance.

Wear Your Helmet and Jacket

It's important to wear a helmet, especially one with a face shield. The shield protects your face from getting struck with hard objects and squirted with liquids. You should also wear a long-sleeved shirt or jacket since protesters use spray bottles to squirt urine and pepper Mace on officers. And as if things weren't bad enough, intelligence reports show that some militant groups are planning on getting AIDS-infected blood to throw on the police.

Concerts

Concerts usually have their own security, uniformed

as well as musclemen in tight T-shirts. They usually do a good job of removing people from the concerts, but there are still situations where you have to go in and arrest someone from a mob of gyrating concertgoers.

The same method used for arresting a skinhead in a crowd of protesters works at a concert. The added element is the music. White power music will psyche the skinheads, intensifying their usual hostility toward you. Therefore, if you can wait until later to get the suspect, perhaps as he leaves, do so. But if you have to get him immediately, do it with enough officers to make the arrest and provide security, then get him out as quickly as you can.

If the concert is taking place in a sports arena or a coliseum, it's a good idea to have a saferoom where prisoners can be taken. The room should be deep within the structure of the site so that passageways to the room can be secured easily by officers. When a subject is arrested, the team only has to move him out of the crowd and to one of the passageways, rather than through the crowd, out the doors, through the parking lot, and to a police car. The prisoner can then be held until the timing is right to move him out.

* * * * *

All the tactical situations presented in this section are basic to dealing with multiple, dangerous subjects and large crowds. The primary difference with skinhead gang members, especially racist skinheads, is their mind-set. Their hate-filled and dangerous beliefs about religion, politics, and race have in some cases been cultivated since early childhood. They are indeed dangerous zealots.

Do not take them lightly.

CHAPTER 16

When a city has an active skinhead population with some level of organization, it's likely its members will hold an occasional rally for some cause or celebration. Martin Luther King's birthday (January 15), Adolph Hitler's birthday (April 20), and White Worker's Day (May 4) are ones on which skinheads almost always assemble to celebrate. Often they will rally side by side with the Ku Klux Klan, which gives both organizations a greater number of participants and an even greater sense of strength.

Whether they act alone or with other white supremacists, their numbers are rarely large, but the problems created at their gatherings are serious, sometimes violent, and often result in injured police officers.

In Washington, D.C., four police officers were injured when violence erupted at a rally of Ku Klux Klan members. More than 2,000 officers were unable to keep peace between 44 Klan marchers and the 3,000 people protesting them.

•

In Cincinnati, Ohio, a fire captain was injured in a clash between 1,500 counterdemonstrators and only six white supremacists.

KEEPING THE PEACE WHEN SKINHEADS RALLY

•

In West Chester, Pennsylvania, a state trooper was injured trying to quell violence between 47 white supremacists and 2,000 spectators. More than 250 officers were on hand during the rally.

•

On several occasions in Portland antiracist skinheads have joined forces with protesters during presidential visits. The antiracist skins stir the crowd and instigate everyone into violent clashes against the police. The violence often goes on for hours, resulting in police injuries and dozens of arrests.

•

In Atlanta, Georgia, 2,500 officers were used to control a march held by just a few white supremacists. Even the large police showing still did not prevent police officers and white supremacists from getting hurt when counter-demonstrators began throwing objects.

The number of demonstrators present at a skins rally may be small, but the problems they cause aren't.

Sometimes there is little or no warning that racist or antiracist skinheads are going to rally. Other times the police will get advance notice, either through intelligence gathering or because the skins will legally obtain a city permit. But even when the police have advance notice, keeping the peace can be a difficult task. At the very least, it's a great logistical challenge that can take weeks of preparation.

Usually, antiracist skinheads join forces with various left-wing groups to rally in favor of or against a cause. The gathering may be a rally, a march, or a protest where the participants carry picket signs and walk in circles on the sidewalk. Although these events require a police presence, they do not cause the same problems the racist skinheads do when they gather. This is primarily because only the presence of the racist skins brings counterdemonstrators. And it's the counterdemonstrators who will cause the most problems.

The following guidelines will help your police agency prepare for a march or rally. Although these suggestions apply to both skinhead factions, they are most applicable to a racist skinhead event.

YOU ARE THE BOSS

- Try to have some control over the particulars of the parade permit, such as the march schedule, route, and what will and will not be allowed along the way. Your purpose is to minimize the potential for violence with counterdemonstrators along the way, but you must be evenhanded in how you do it.
- Identify the leaders and communicate with them prior to and during the event.
- Don't impose restrictions that you would not do with other groups. Remember, it's not illegal to be a skinhead.
- The white supremacists will be looking for unfairness from ZOG, and if they find it, more problems may result.

- Try not to allow rallies during and at any other public demonstration.
- Racist skinheads may want to rally on Martin Luther King Day, but you should prevent it if they want to do it where others are celebrating the event.
- In the interest of public safety, you are justified in telling skinheads when and where they can rally.
- You can also tell them in what formation they can march, and you can limit the time and the location where they hold their speeches.
- Have an ending time so you can order them to disperse after the permit expires.
- Have the option to terminate the march if trouble arises.
- Make sure there is a clause in the ordinance preventing marchers from possessing weapons. The definition of a weapon should be clear: firearms, slugging instruments, explosives, stabbing instruments, etc.

USE YOUR COMMUNITY POLICING

- Inform minority community leaders of the event and ensure them it will be handled with a strict and sufficient police presence. Ask them to spread the word that the skinheads are expressing their freedom of speech, and the best way for the community to react is to ignore them.

ENLIST HELP FROM OTHER POLICE AGENCIES

- Plan your work schedules so you have a maximum number of officers available.
- Borrow from other local jurisdictions if you need to beef up your numbers.
- Use officers from other jurisdictions who can identify specific skinheads or gangs.
- Inform county, state, and federal agencies of the event.

Involvement by other agencies may stroke the collective ego of the skinheads, but it will also send a message to them

A demonstration can easily get out of control if you do not establish early on that you are in charge.

that you are ready for whatever they want to do. Counter-demonstrators will also see the formidable presence and may think twice before they act out on their emotions.

INTELLIGENCE GATHERING

- If skinheads are coming from another city or state, call those jurisdictions to find out what they know about their gangs, specific individuals, and tactics they may employ.
- Get as much information on the parade application as possible: names of the organizers and names of the organizations (gangs) participating.
- Gather intelligence in the left-wing community. Since counterdemonstators are frequently the instigators, it's important to know what groups and the names of any specific individuals planning to protest. Hint: It's usually the same militant left-wing types who protest everything.

KNOW THE ROUTE

- If the rally is taking place in a park, make sure park employees are aware.
- Any private residences that may be affected should be informed of the pending gathering.
- If it's a downtown march, contact businesses and agencies on the route and inform them of the event, as well as of any traffic and parking restrictions.
- Any potential targets along the route or elsewhere should be warned, such as synagogues; gay districts; and black, Asian, and Jewish businesses.
- Develop a parking plan and decide where barriers will be set up. Arrange to get a parking lot for police cars, arrest teams, and booking and jail transportation.
- Establish a way to keep the skinheads separated from the counterdemonstrators: police tape, barricades, a line of uniformed officers.
- Restrict spectators with carefully drawn police lines.

Allow only police and press near the skinheads.
- Require the press to have legitimate credentials.
- Try not to let anyone join the march after it has begun.

OFFICER PREPARATION

- Create an outline of schedules and duties for uniformed officers and specialized units.
- Hold as many briefings as necessary with representatives from the units to share all new information.
- Conduct one briefing immediately after you get solid information about the event and another the day before the event.
- Discuss the groups and individuals participating.
- Distribute photos of people of interest.
- Assign new police duties as they arise and go step by step through the event to ensure that all units understand their assignments.
- Tell officers to expect abuse from the marchers and counterdemonstrators. They should expect the white supremacists to taunt them in their speeches and call them race traitors and ZOG puppets. They may try to provoke the officers into a physical confrontation. The officers should expect even more abuse from the counterdemonstrators, whose mass may contain certain individuals highly skilled at inciting both sides to violence.

CONTROLLING THE VIOLENCE

- Use K-9 units or bomb-disposal units to check for explosives at potential target areas along the march route and at the rally point.
- Assign officers to look for suspicious people and cars along the route, especially on parallel side streets. Pay special note to people with backpacks.
- Station sniper units on roof tops.
- Helicopter observation should begin prior to the march or rally.

Police maintain a line between racist and antiracist protestors at the same demonstration.

- Officers working intersections should shut off streets and set up barricades.
- Assign officers to photograph and videotape the activities.
- Undercover officers should be in place.
- Set up a command post with radios, telephones, and representatives from all units.
- The arrest teams, custody bus, and officers in holding should all be in place.

DEBRIEF

- Representatives from each of the units should attend a debriefing.
- Discuss what went wrong and what was done well.
- Update new intelligence and make sure all participating agencies get the information.
- Learn from your mistakes.

CHAPTER 17

Some skinheads drop out of sight because they have moved away, gone to prison in some other jurisdiction, or gone straight and no longer draw police attention. We hear from time to time about a skinhead who has left the movement and the philosophy, but inevitably he will reappear on the scene a few months later.

JASON

Jason is one who has successfully made the break. He was in the skins for two years and got out just before his gang brutally murdered a black man. He initially got into a skinhead gang because he wanted to be tough and associate with others who had a reputation for being tough. "At first," he says, "we didn't hate anyone. We were just a bunch of guys who liked to fight." They would cruise the streets together picking on people of every race, creed, and color.

Then as time went by, Jason's group began to develop a philosophy, the result of meeting a skinhead from an upper-echelon white supremacy organization. The skinhead brought with him a strict set of neo-Nazi, racist beliefs that were accepted by the gang wholeheartedly. Many of the beliefs already existed among some of the gang members, but after they learned a

TWO SKINHEADS WHO GOT OUT

219

formalized version of white supremacy, Jason and his friends became more ideologically motivated. "We just basically thought as a group," he says.

The experienced skinhead's teaching was the driving force behind how the gang began to act. He was charismatic and somewhat famous for having been on television; the newly recruited skinheads wanted to impress him. "He was a big deal," Jason says. The skinhead teacher would initiate the action, and the student skinheads would roll along with it. Over the next three months, they committed dozens of unprovoked assaults on whites and minorities.

"There was something called a 'pride test,'" Jason says. "When you didn't do something the group agreed to, you got beat up."

The gang often handed out racist literature around the city. What bothered Jason later, after he had left the gang and began to think about his experience, was that he never heard any objections to the literature. In fact, many "normal types" gave encouragement to the skinheads. "It was incredible how many people agreed with us," Jason says.

As the weeks rolled by, Jason began to question what he was doing. One night, they went out and committed three unrelated assaults, each time beating the victims to the ground. During one of the assaults, Jason's gang was shot at, an experience that made him have even more second thoughts about whether or not he wanted to continue his involvement in the violence.

About a month later, Jason left the gang, and a month after that his buddies killed a black man. "I couldn't believe my friends could do something like that," Jason says. "And I couldn't believe the guy died."

His surprise was typical of many gang members who have been close to a killing. Apparently, it never occurs to them that kicking people in the head and beating them with hard objects just might end their lives.

Later, Jason felt ashamed of what he had been involved with. He was beginning to associate with blacks and, for the first time, saw them as people, not much different from him. "I began to understand things."

He also began to see himself differently. He realized the only emotion he had been able to show had been rage. He looked hard at himself and vowed to never fight again.

For a while, he visited high school classes and told them his story. He warned them to stay away from drugs and racist gangs. He even worked in the black community doing volunteer work on elderly people's homes.

At this writing, he has been out of the skins for four years.

Jason's story is one of the few where a gang member has successfully left his violent life-style. As is the case in other gangs, skinheads don't always find it easy to leave. It's not uncommon for an ex-skinhead to be assaulted and harassed for years after leaving. Those remaining in the gang accuse them of being traitors or informants for the police.

GREG WITHROW

One ex-skinhead has taken his harrowing story on the talk show circuit and before community groups. Greg Withrow claims to be the founder of the Aryan Youth Movement, a now defunct branch of Tom Metzger's WAR organization. His defection from the world of hate resulted in his crucifiction by the same skinheads he once led.

He tells of his father, a 6-foot, 4-inch domineering man who ruled his household. The father raised him to "lead the white race," Withrow says. "Some fathers raise their kids to be doctors, lawyers, or ballerinas. I was raised to be some sort of 'führer.'"

After joining WAR, he enrolled at Sacramento's American River College, where he formed the White Student Union. His advisor was Tom Metzger, who gave him money and encouragement. In his role as the union's self-appointed leader, Withrow recruited new members into what subsequently became WAR's Aryan Youth Movement.

Withrow also organized the Sacramento Area

Skinheads, a gang actively involved in drinking, narcotics, and assault. Many of the events he participated in were so despicable to him he still will not talk about them. (Perhaps he is waiting for the statute of limitations to run out.)

He went on to garner a lengthy police record for his activities and did a little prison time. In 1986 his father died, which would be Greg Withrow's last summer of hate.

"I honored my father," Withrow says. "When he died it hurt, but there was also a sense of relief. I actually began to feel for the first time. I had this thought that maybe I didn't have to carry this on anymore. Then I thought, *No, no, no, it's my duty. I must carry on my duty. Honor my family, my ancestors, my race, my nation.* I just kept forgetting to honor myself." Withrow continued with this internal struggle until finally he decided to pay Tom Metzger a visit to tell him he wanted out of the racist movement. Metzger became furious, and the other skinheads made life unbearable for him.

When he finally grew tired of all the harassment from his "friends," he decided to go public and announce that he was going to quit white supremacy for good. Although he made his announcement on several California television shows, he was to discover that getting out was not going to be easy.

On August 8, 1987, Withrow reported that a group of skinheads, including his best friend, ambushed him outside a bar, beating him and slashing his throat with a razor. Then they drove nails through his palms, pinning him, crucifixion style, to an 8-foot-wide board. They left him lying near a Dumpster, where, ironically, a black couple stopped to help after several whites had ignored him and walked on by.

He now tells his story to young people, some of the same ones he tried to recruit into his organization years ago.

Racial violence is not going away. Informed observers predict that racial tension and explosive racial violence are going to be with us for the entire decade and, in fact, may not peak until the end of the century. Already in the first three years of the 1990s, bias-motivated murders are showing a steady increase: 20 in 1990, 27 in 1991, and 31 in 1992. Other hate crimes are up too: cross burnings up 16 percent and vandalism up 49 percent. As alarming as these statistics are, they are most likely conservative, given the fact that many hate crimes are not reported, and, unfortunately, many crimes are not even recognized as being motivated by bias.

Failure to report hate crimes has always been a problem. Victims refuse to report an incident for many reasons:

- Fear of retaliation
- Belief the police will be unable to do anything about it
- Belief the police will sympathize with the perpetrator
- Fear of bringing unwanted attention to themselves
- View that the crime "goes with the territory"
- Denial of the existence of hate crimes

Only through education by the police and community organiza-

RACIAL VIOLENCE IS NOT GOING AWAY

tions will more victims be willing to come forward.

Many school boards and administrators refuse to acknowledge hate crimes on their campuses. While talking with a high school principal on an unrelated matter, I asked if he had any skinhead students attending his school. He vigorously shook his head and, in a tone that indicated his disgust, said he would never allow such a thing on his campus, nor would he allow any student to wear gang attire. As I left his office and stepped into the hall, I literally bumped into a skinhead, who was attired in Doc Martens and flight jacket and had a shaved head.

Gerald Arenberg, executive director of the National Association of Chiefs of Police in Miami, Florida, said that college and university officials often attempt to cover up campus crimes rather than deal with them. Most crimes of harassment and graffiti are not reported because administrators and even some campus security people are reluctant to acknowledge they occurred.

"Education officials don't want to admit that hate crimes and prejudice exist in their own special worlds," Arenburg said.

The National Institute against Prejudice and Violence (NIAPV) projects that 25 percent of minority college students will be victimized by racial violence, and 25 percent of those victims will be victimized a second time. When the NIAPV tried to conduct a study on the secondary-level schools similar to the one conducted on colleges, it was unsuccessful because no school district would agree to sponsor the project. The director of the research effort, Howard Ehrlich, said, "My experience has been that if it is anything controversial, the school administrators try to avoid it."

When administrators are complacent about racial tension and bias crimes on their campuses, they are creating a fertile ground where violence can happen. A recent poll showed that 25 percent of high school seniors have been threatened with violence. In 1991, 900 teachers were threatened and 40 were assaulted each hour on school property. The most startling statistics show that one out of 20 students brings a gun to school. In Portland, some parents give their children guns to take to school for their own protection.

With these things already happening, the setting is ripe for racial violence. Administrators cannot bury their heads in the sand. A strong response is essential to show perpetrators that they cannot get away with their activities, and that future incidents will not be tolerated.

WHITES ARE NOT THE ONLY PERPETRATORS

When examining bias crimes, the tendency is to think in terms of white on black: white racist skinheads assaulting a lone black man or hooded Klansmen lynching a black from a tree. Though that is the image, the truth is that other races commit racially motivated crimes too.

Of the 58 hate murders documented by Klanwatch in 1991 and 1992, 41 were racially motivated. Seventeen were black on white, and 13 were white on black.

Indeed, hate crimes are committed by all groups: Hispanic on white, Asian on white, black on Jews, etc. Some observers believe that black-on-white crimes are on a definite increase.

Rap singer Sister Souljah argues that blacks cannot be racists because their status as a minority means they have no power. Other blacks justify their racist violence with the excuse they are fighting back against years of oppression and taking revenge for years of slavery.

Well, the perpetrators can make that argument to a judge, but the fact remains that a bias crime is a bias crime regardless of the motive.

In cases involving minorities committing racially motivated crimes, once again denial rears its head high. Some police administrators want the issue played down for fear of rattling the minority community. The cases get worked, but little or no mention is made of them.

The media rarely report black-on-white stories for the same reason. I frequently get calls from reporters asking for information about racial assaults or statistics on bias crimes. When I begin to provide them with information about black-on-white racial incidents, knowing full well that is not what they want, I enjoy listening to them sputter and cough and say they only want white-on-black incidents. Some reporters make the pretense of taking notes about black-on-white cases, but that angle is never covered in their stories.

HATE CRIME LEGISLATION UNDER THE GUN

Forty-seven states have legislation that targets crimes committed based on a person's race, religion, or sexual orientation. However, First Amendment concerns are picking away at those pieces of legislation.

Critics of bias-crime laws claim that they violate rights of free speech and expression. A recent Supreme Court decision struck down a St. Paul, Minnesota, ordinance that banned cross burnings, swastika displays, and other similar expressions of bigotry. A Wisconsin court struck down that state's bias-crime law because it "punished thought and chilled free speech." Similar laws in Michigan, Vermont, Oregon, and New York have thus far been upheld.

WHERE IS IT ALL HEADING?

Racially motivated crimes committed by all races will continue into the new century, most likely increasing each year.

Racist skinheads are just part of the problem, but they are the most obvious symbol of racial hatred. They dress to flaunt who they are and what they believe in, and, unlike other races, they are organized for it. Racism is the illness, and skinheads are its festering boils. As long as there are societal conditions that create this hatred, we will have skinheads with us. But they will thrive only where they are tolerated or where there is ignorance as to who they are.

Law enforcement must know what skinheads are

about. I hope this book has been of some help in defining the groups and their objectives.

Knowledge is power.

about. I hope this book has been of some help in defining the groups and their objectives.

Knowledge is power.

Loren W. Christensen joined the U.S. Army in 1967 and served as a military policeman stateside and in Vietnam. In 1972, he joined the Portland Police Bureau in Oregon, where he has worked a variety of jobs, including street patrol, juveniles, dignitary protection, police academy instructor, and radio dispatcher. Christensen began working skinhead gangs in 1988 and is currently assigned to the Gang Enforcement Team, where he is a recognized authority on skinheads and white supremacy crimes.

Christensen has written six books on the martial arts and a textbook about runaways for teenagers. He has also written dozens of articles for a variety of magazines.